KASEY NORTON

SOJOURNER

Dedication

This tiny book is dedicated to the God who has pursued me for over 4 decades. No matter how hard I've tried to squirm out of His grasp, He's always been right there to show me His nail-pierced hands are tender and that He'd never take something I'd be better off having. This book is a pitiful offering but, in this moment, it's the best I have to give. I lay it before Him and ask that He use my experiences for as much good as possible.

Preface

As I sit down to the write this, the rain is pounding on our tile roof. It's a pleasing sound a little like white noise in our otherwise just plain *noisy* life. Repairs that had been made last week to prevent the rainwater from pouring into the house didn't take. Water is surging right through the kitchen ceiling and the floor is covered in splashes and puddles. I should probably be more irritated by the mess than I am.

As we laid the children down for sleep tonight, we found ourselves hugging three who hadn't been here last night and who aren't mentioned in this book. Because God does the unexpected like that. He knows the law, and our limits, yet sometimes He asks us to get creative about how we navigate both. Today pushed us over the threshold … we now have more Thai children than American. We started the day 8-6 and ended it 9-8. It happened so fast, with pretty much no warning, and yet somehow it's going to work out. Out of our 17 children only two aren't in Thailand with us. We currently have a total of 24 mouths to feed every day, and that's just the people who live here. That number doesn't include those God's given us to feed each day who *don't*. I should probably be more concerned about the money than I am.

We're out of space and had to move three kids into our room

today. We're out of time to get approval for our little school. We're out of all our English students at The Mission Post, save two, thanks to covid. We're out of energy and brainpower and know-how and grit. But we're not out of desire to serve Jesus.

And so as the rain sneaks inside our house, where God has provided refuge for so many, we are grateful. Grateful to be counted worthy so we might labor for His cause. Grateful to be able to give our children an experience so few ever have. Grateful to get to leave fingerprints on the beautiful people around us. Grateful to struggle, or even suffer from exhaustion, for our good and His glory.

This little book went from idea to reality in less than two weeks and, because we didn't want to waste money paying someone to edit, you may well find more than a few typographical errors. Kindly overlook them knowing my eyes grew too tired to read my own writing a single more time.

Also forgive the insertion of emotion regarding how much I miss my boys in America. One thing editing this little project taught me was that I mentioned them a few times. :)

You can follow our journey through our website at https://walk ingredeemed.com. There you will find blog posts, Bible studies, tools and resources.

You can financially support our ministries here in Thailand in one of two ways:
    1) Make a purchase through our online store which offers our digital resources and books, as well as a line of Christian t-shirts

we've designed. You can find it at <u>shopwalkingredeemed.com</u>

2) Donate through the links found on the <u>donate page</u> of our website. There are various ways you can choose to do it and this pages offers links to them all.

Please know how grateful we are for every single prayer whispered on behalf of the work on this continent. Not just for *our* projects, but for all those God has moving and growing to reach the greatest number of people possible before time truly runs out.

* * *

One

Give, and it shall be given unto you; good measure, pressed down, and shaken together, and running over, shall men give into your bosom. For with the same measure that ye mete withal it shall be measured to you again. Luke 6:38

We'd gotten an unexpected sum of money. It was substantial and we felt excitement surge through us as we considered all the ways the money could be put to use. Over the following week or so, God opened up avenues for us to not only proceed with the development of the children's home and school, but to bless others besides. The amount quickly dwindled, but there was still enough to get a solid start on our next big expansion project.

Several days passed and the calendar flipped a page. The new month brought with it the clear message that the money we had left wasn't sufficient to start the construction on the dormitory, as planned. We'd have to use it to sustain the current work and provide for those under our care. Disappointment settled over me.

As one day blurred into the next, I experienced a silencing of the voice of God. My morning worship times turned into a struggle just to get up. And when I did finally drag myself out of bed, it was to meet with what felt like a stone wall. I heard nothing. I felt empty.

After about a week of this, during which time I was also up in the nights caring for a sickly child, I had my fill and wanted no more of the silence. The verses from Romans 8:35-39 came to mind and I was reminded that literally *nothing* can separate us from God … unless we give permission for it to do so.

Humbled, I owned that the breakdown in relationship was my own doing. God had never turned His face from me. I'd allowed a simple circumstance that hadn't gone my way, to cause me to feel rejected by Him; I'd been the one to turn away.

The following morning I practically jerked myself out of bed. It was well before dawn and I sat in the quiet, reading a portion of Scripture. I read until I knew God had spoken to the worn places in my heart and then I got up and went out to prayer walk. As I made my way around the rice paddy, the verse from Luke 6:28 came to mind and I was immediately convicted. It says:

And though I bestow all my goods to feed the poor, and though I give my body to be burned, and have not charity, it profiteth me nothing.
1 Corinthians 13:3

I wanted to give the money we had the way *I* wanted to give it. I wanted it to do what *I* wanted it to do. But I was also struck by the fact that I wanted to give of our money instead of my *self*. God was calling me higher. Yes, He wants us to be unselfish stewards of all the financial resources He gives us. But even more than that, He wants us to be faithful stewards of our time, energy, patience, compassion, love, and kindness.

It's easier to give money.

I was rebuked that morning and I'm grateful God had softened my heart to receive the rebuking. Because it's when I've emptied myself of *everything*, drained to the dregs and holding nothing back, that I'll find the greatest blessings being poured out. Blessing and provision that He then, in turn, wants me to again pour onto others. You cannot outgive God. It's been said so many times it's almost lost its impact. We know it, but often don't truly believe it. We think we have to hold a little in reserve.

If we do, however, we can expect God will also hold back that which He longs to be able to give us!

Discussion prompt: Are you trying to serve God in your own ways rather than surrendering yourself entirely to His leading, no matter where it takes you?

Two

Ye have not yet resisted unto blood, striving against sin. And ye have forgotten the exhortation which speaketh unto you as unto children, My son, despise not thou the chastening of the Lord, nor faint when thou art rebuked of him: For whom the Lord loveth he chasteneth, and scourgeth every son whom he receiveth. If ye endure chastening, God dealeth with you as with sons; for what son is he whom the father chasteneth not? Hebrews 12:4–8

Ah, the waters that get muddied by shouts of legalism. Because somewhere along the way, Christians have bought into the lie that obedience *is* legalism.

This reprehensible deceit from the enemy has drawn us into the quicksand of a pick-your-truth-because-anything-goes understanding of the gospel. We're suddenly a collective church confused by simple things like how many genders there really are.

And the reality is, many of us are raising soft Christians. We love our children more than words and yet we're modeling destructive behavior to them, teaching them it's okay to pick and choose which of God's instructions we want to adopt into our lifestyle.

This is why we have a generation of young adults turning their backs on the gospel and it's why the youth of today have little interest in buying what we're selling.

If God said it, it IS a command. It's up to us to study it for ourselves, but only after first praying for the Holy Spirit to give us the discernment to understand. Too many of us are basing our Christian experience, or lack thereof, on those around us.

But let's be honest here, and not just toss around words, regardless of how true they may be. Because obedience comes with a price. In that verse from Hebrews 12 we read that the price is blood, which is symbolic of a death to self.

I can't live, embracing my natural desires, and call myself a Christ follower. That's hypocrisy. In a world that's determined to tell us to give ourselves grace, and still more grace, I'm going to boldly suggest we already give ourselves way too much of it.

It's not the holding of oneself to a Biblical standard that drives people to despair and suicide. It's the living in conflict with our own consciences that does it. We're literally killing ourselves, and our children, to teach them a Christless gospel. Nobody can survive religion because religion demands without giving and gives without demanding.

James 1:22 says, *But be ye doers of the word, and not hearers only, deceiving your own selves.*

It's interesting, though, how those who have entered into this abiding and obedient experience with Christ just seem a little odd to the casual observer. Or they somehow make the less eager disciples a bit uncomfortable. Because the law is simply a mirror that allows us to check our reflection aside God's. Standing next to someone who's reflecting more intentionally just makes us feel dull and dirty, and we prefer not to be around people like that.

The only way we will find the victory, is to put our whole selves, *every drop of energy*, into pursuing the heart of God. Because as we do, He'll inscribe His law even deeper into our hearts so it's not a list of rules we're trying to follow, but rather an umbrella of safety we dare not run out from under.

We need to thank Him for the chastening because without it, we'd never find the courage to endure the battle of resistance the enemy is constantly waging.

Discussion prompt: What areas of your life do you find yourself choosing to walk in opposition to counsel God provides through His holy Word? Have you grown to equate total obedience with legalism?

Three

Take fast hold of instruction; let her not go: keep her; for she is thy life.
Proverbs 4:13

How many times have you heard it said, or even said it yourself, something like, "I wish life came with an instruction manual."? Well, there's good news … it does!

Have you ever read the verses found in Ephesians 4:22-32? They are life verses that encapsulate pretty much the entire Christian experience. Let's read them together:

That ye put off concerning the former conversation the old man, which is corrupt according to the deceitful lusts;
And be renewed in the spirit of your mind;
And that ye put on the new man, which after God is created in righteousness and true holiness.
Wherefore putting away lying, speak every man truth with his neighbour: for we are members one of another.
Be ye angry, and sin not: let not the sun go down upon your wrath:

Neither give place to the devil.
Let him that stole steal no more: but rather let him labour, working
with his hands the thing which is good, that he may have to give to
him that needeth.
Let no corrupt communication proceed out of your mouth, but that
which is good to the use of edifying, that it may minister grace unto
the hearers.
And grieve not the holy Spirit of God, whereby ye are sealed unto
the day of redemption.
Let all bitterness, and wrath, and anger, and clamour, and evil
speaking, be put away from you, with all malice:
And be ye kind one to another, tenderhearted, forgiving one another,
even as God for Christ's sake hath forgiven you.
If you're a true seeker after instruction, you've just read the words
which throw light on the way in which God wants us to walk.

It's all in there: Putting away self, allowing Christ to robe you in His righteousness, speaking truth, learning to be angry *without* sinning, laboring for that which we need so we can help *others*, controlling the tongue, abhorring the very *idea* of grieving the Spirit of God, being kind and forgiving to others, as He has been to us.

It's the embodiment of surrender. It's death to self. It's the taking **fast hold of instruction**.

But if it's so simple, why do we find it so hard? The truth is ugly so brace yourself. It's hard because we love sinning. We're addicted to it, even. We love self and the setting aside of her (or him) is painful and costly. We always hear salvation is free but that doesn't mean it's cheap.

Just this morning, Robbie and I wanted to slip away on the motorbike for an incredibly brief "date". We were just planning to ride into town because the morning offered a reprieve from the intense heat. We were going to come straight back so he could get a few of the kids to the dentist. We rarely get away and friends from America keep reminding us we need to.

However, the morning was slow getting rolling with the children, and by the time we were leaving, we realized that somehow we'd skipped family worship. For a minute we were going to just have the older girls lead it, as we do when something demands we be away. But as we were walking out, the Spirit spoke and by the mercy of God, we took *fast hold of instruction* and went back in the living room to call our brood together.

We *know* the command to bring our family before the altar. We know the need to put God before all else and let Him stretch time when it's needed. Through obedience to the revealed will of God, we were able to meet our responsibility, and still have sufficient time to get away quickly.

It wasn't long but it was refreshing in a way I know it wouldn't have been if we'd turned our backs on the instructions God had given.

I'm thankful we didn't.

Discussion prompt: Is God giving you instructions that you'd rather not hear? What is your response in these times?

Four

Who shall ascend into the hill of the Lord? or who shall stand in his holy place?He that hath clean hands, and a pure heart; who hath not lifted up his soul unto vanity, nor sworn deceitfully. He shall receive the blessing from the Lord, and righteousness from the God of his salvation. Psalm 24:3-5

If you're old enough to remember back to the days when only the top three in a race got a prize, you know we experienced a time unlike the present. An inclusive society should simply mean that everyone matters equally; apparently it's being seen as meaning everyone is *rewarded* equally.

Gone are the days where greater effort yields greater gain. Unless, that is, you're a Christian.

And before you write me off as a legalist, give me a moment to clarify. I'm not saying we can work our way to heaven, I'm saying we can *abide* our way there. But abiding takes discipline and the sacrifice of carnal desire. It requires that our energy and effort be put into fastening our eyes on Jesus, but what we gain as a result is without measure.

We're living in a society where even much of the church has adopted this anything-goes theology. We're far more afraid of offending people than we are of offending God. The church is on a downward spiral into the depths of preaching a feel-good theology with little Biblical basis, though it's possibly never been so involved in humanitarian efforts and causes.

We've extracted, in large measure, the Redeemer from the redemption. It's an empty gospel when we try to usurp His place in the story.

Scripture tells us that not all who claim to be Christian will be saved. Matthew 7:21-23 issues a sharp warning that few find pleasant to consider: *Not every one that saith unto me, Lord, Lord, shall enter into the kingdom of heaven; but he that doeth the will of my Father which is in heaven. Many will say to me in that day, Lord, Lord, have we not prophesied in thy name? and in thy name have cast out devils? and in thy name done many wonderful works? And then will I profess unto them, I never knew you: depart from me, ye that work iniquity.*

Our lives have been granted to us with the gift of free will and we can choose how we want to live them. And while, in the end we will each receive our "reward", the same one will not be given to all.

For some reason, that rubs a little. It doesn't fit the narrative trending in the world. Nobody wants to be told they're doing wrong, or living in a way they shouldn't, or that the habits they so cherish are in direct contradiction to the character of God. That's called being exclusive or intolerant or bigoted. And to be fair, the vast majority of us probably run ahead of the Spirit when trying to help lead a wayward friend or family member to the straight path. Those occasions represent a statistical nightmare that has proven very hard to reverse.

Having clean hands and a pure heart requires a continual surrender. A daily decision that I must decrease so He can increase. A humbling of self so we can see we have nothing to offer but filthy rags without being robed in His righteousness. I want to receive the blessing from the Lord rather than leading a life that exempts me from that blessing.

But we must always be aware that how we truly live matters more than what we simply profess.

Discussion prompt: Are there things you're clinging to, refusing to heed the quiet voice to your conscience, that are keeping you from abiding with Christ? Are you unintentionally buying into the myth that, since God loves everyone, a profession of faith is good enough? Do you hear God calling you higher and deeper?

Five

And the Word became flesh, and dwelt among us, (and we beheld his glory, the glory as of the only begotten of the Father) full of grace and truth. 1 John 1:14

Back when I was in junior high and high school, my brothers and I would return from school to an empty house and it was our responsibility to put things in order. The mornings were always rushed as we slept until the last possible minute and then had to race to the bus stop before we missed our ride. The house was left in disarray which bothered nobody until we returned, when we instantly regretted the earlier haste.

I've always preferred things neat and tidy, and I detest clutter, so I'd faithfully go to work getting things cleaned up. My brothers, however, weren't nearly so motivated. One was three years older than me while the other was three years younger.

My older brother, Bob, developed the distasteful habit of coming in, throwing himself on the couch and watching the popular sitcoms airing on cable for teens. As if that wasn't irritating enough, he'd also ask me to serve him things like drinks or snacks. I loved him and so I'd often submit to his wishes. Until one day, I'd had enough of having my role in his life misunderstood. I wasn't placed there to serve his every whim, and the time had come to help him grasp that.

He was once again sprawled on the couch watching tv while I was doing all the work. Realizing his happiness could only be improved upon if he had a sandwich, *that he didn't have to make himself*, he called out asking me to bring him one. Not missing a beat, I sweetly agreed.

I proceeded to make him the kind of sandwich he liked best, only I decided it needed the addition of one small, unexpected topping to really make it special. And so I pulled the horseradish from the fridge and smathered both pieces of bread liberally with the spicy spread. Grinning, I closed it up, delivered it to my beloved brother, and then quickly walked away so he wouldn't see me laugh.

Not a minute passed before I heard him shout and I walked over to the doorway and leaned against it smugly. He looked at me with watery eyes as he tried desperately to cool his nasal passages which were burning like wildfire. I'm not recommending my approach, but he did learn his lesson that I wasn't his servant.

When Jesus came to this earth, the Word had quite literally become flesh. He lived among the people with singleness of purpose … to show them the Father. The glory of God was on full display through the life of the Son, and it was there for all to behold. Yet, nobody truly understood His purpose.

Not even His disciples. Maybe even *especially* His disciples.

They were looking for a Savior from Roman oppression, much the way the world now is looking for someone to save them from overreaching government policies. They wanted temporal relief so badly they didn't understand *that* wasn't His purpose in coming.

HIs purpose was so much greater.

It's easy to look back, from our vantage point, and wonder how they could be so blind. They had Jesus right in front of them and could behold His glory as He healed the broken in body, and in spirit. But are we any better?

Are we still misunderstanding His role in our lives? Are we picking and choosing when we want to involve Him, expecting *Him* to do *our* bidding instead of the reverse?

It's a dangerous limb to perch on and yet so many have gathered there that the branch is about to break and the church appears ready to collapse. However, we know from history, that God has preserved a people, in all ages, through the pure and unadulterated gospel. It's only as we're immersed in His word, and seated in His presence, that we will truly glimpse His glory, *the glory as of the only begotten of the Father, full of grace and truth.*

I, like Moses, want to be pleading to be hid in the cleft of the rock so He can pass before me. And I want even *that* not to be enough, because I want to *want more than anything* the unfettered desire to dwell with Him daily.

Discussion prompt: Are there ways in which your selfish desires have risen, causing you to misunderstand God's purpose as it pertains to your life?

Six

For though we walk in the flesh, we do not war after the flesh: (For the weapons of our warfare are not carnal, but mighty through God to the pulling down of strongholds;) Casting down imaginations, and every high thing that exalteth itself against the knowledge of God, and bringing into captivity every thought to the obedience of Christ.
2 Corinthians 10:3-5

I didn't grow up in church and, by the time I reached early adulthood, I'd only ever been seated in a pew a handful of times. So when I encountered God at the age of 18 and was baptized, I jumped into Christianity with both feet. I wanted to be as good as I could possibly be.

The problem I quickly discovered, however, was that I was very bad at being good.

I was engaged at 19, married at 20, and holding my first baby a week after I turned 21. It was a whirlwind but that first little boy, with the big eyes and infectious smile, awakened within me an intense longing to be godly. And so I threw myself, full force, into reforming my ways. I was well-intentioned but I quickly found my focus had shifted from Christ to *self*.

I studied Scripture for the sole purpose of learning what I should and shouldn't be doing. There was no reform too bold, as far as I was concerned, since my primary goal was to outwardly *look* the part of a Christ follower. But beyond that, I tried reforming everyone in my family right along with me.

And as I added 4 more babies over the following 6 years, I dragged each one into my misguided quest. To the casual observer, I apparently looked fairly pulled together. To my family, I most certainly was not. Where there's an absence of long-suffering, and gentleness, and goodness, and joy there's an obvious absence of Christ.

So my first 5 children were raised in *religion*, which is a bondage from which Jesus came to set the captives free.

I was re-shackling them without realizing it and the result was an insidious distaste for what they were taught to *believe* was a Christian lifestyle. If only I had understood, all those years ago, that I was warring after the flesh. I was doing things *my* way, in my *own* strength.

The truth of the matter is, reform begins on our knees. It begins as we sit, like Martha's Mary, before the feet of Jesus. As we learn who He is, why He came, and why He's coming back. And it begins as we come to grasp what He's asking us to do *until* He returns. That concept of *abiding* is His chosen weapon of our warfare and it's mighty enough to pull down strongholds no amount of grit ever could.

Living out the fullness of today's Scripture verse means praying for God to give us the willingness to allow the Spirit to *take every thought captive to the obedience of Christ*. Have you ever committed an entire day to not only filtering your words and actions through the Holy Spirit, but even your *thoughts*? If you have, you know it takes commitment and the determination to keep letting Him dust you off after you slip back into old thought patterns. Because we aren't naturally skilled gatekeepers of the mind. It takes practice and an indwelling of the Spirit who saves us from ourselves.

God has been merciful to me, and has given me additional opportunities to raise children in a knowledge of the character of God. It's been sloppy and I get it wrong more than I get it right. But the fruit is children who gravitate to that which is good instead of children who've been conditioned to sneak toward the *not-so-good* as soon as my head is turned. I crippled my first five children with a false gospel and, though I did it unknowingly, the consequence is the same. I'm watching God lead all my beautiful oldest children, but I created an additional battle for them I deeply regret them having to face.

We can't put our efforts into *performing* or we'll slip so deep into the role that we'll miss the Director. The energy and focus must be on basking in His presence so that our prayers and cooperation pull down strongholds.

Anything else is like trying to run in quicksand.

Discussion prompt: Have you ever fallen into the pit of

legalism? What strongholds need pulled down in your life or in the lives of your family? How committed are you to learning to abide?

Seven

And not only so, but we glory in tribulations also: knowing that tribulation worketh patience; patience, experience; and experience, hope. Romans 5:3-4

The day had been a good one. A lot had been accomplished at home, things went well at The Mission Post, and our student count was increasing in spite of new covid concerns. Every child who walks into that office gives the Spirit a chance to reach them and their families and so we were thrilled.

Nikolas and Hannah had returned to the house in high spirits and, as we gathered with all the Children's Home staff for worship that evening, a peace settled over the place. I like those times.

They're my favorite.

Following worship, Robbie and I got into the truck with our monk friend, Ram, who'd spent the day on our property with the water buffalo he keeps here. He didn't have a ride back into the temple so we were providing him one. The kids were tucked into bed and I hugged Nik goodnight because he was headed back to his house in town soon.

Exhausted from the productive day, I stretched out across the back seat and fell asleep as we bumped down the road. I was awakened after a short time by the closing of the truck door and I looked up to see we were at the temple and Robbie was on the phone.

I moved to the front seat, which Ram had vacated, just as Robbie finished the call. He pressed his hand to his forehead and said, "Nik wrecked on the motorbike."

One of my worst fears was playing out in real time.

"Is he hurt?" I asked quickly. Robbie nodded his head *no* but we called Nik back anyway to verify. And then we headed out to find him somewhere along the dark road between town and our house.

It was a quiet ride and my thoughts were all over the place. We finally spotted him, perched on his battered bike, in a dark stretch of road. Pulling over, we jumped out to access his injuries.

To my relief, I could confirm with my own eyes that he hadn't been badly hurt and he explained that a stray dog had cut in front of him. With the low light, he hadn't seen the dog until it was too late and then he jammed on the brakes and locked them up. There's a learning curve to using two wheels for transportation, that much is clear.

The bike wouldn't run so we grabbed a rope from the back of the truck and Robbie got on the bike holding the rope so I could pull him with the truck the rest of the way home. Nik got his wounds cleaned and we got him back home to shower.

As the moment of intensity passed, I was able to reflect and truly praise God for His mercy. I don't know why we get so few uneventful days. I don't know why our kids seem to pick up one virus after another and then stay sick for weeks. I don't know why the children we've taken in to love and care for still sometimes scream that they hate us and want to leave. I don't know why the enemy seems so intent on harassing us, but I do know this: *God knows.*

And He knows that if we'll only *glory also in tribulation*, our patience for hard times will increase.

And as we learn to endure through the rough patches, we'll also learn to stop wishing them away because we'll understand that, while they don't feel good, they're adding experience into our lives that God will use for good in the future.

And as we build a portfolio of experience, and we're filing away in our hearts the ways in which God has led, we'll find ourselves the beneficiary of the kind of hope that begets peace and rest.

God understands our desire to be bathed in those times of peace. And He wants us to revel in them. But ultimately, He's trying to teach us to praise Him in *all* things and in *every* circumstance.

He wants us to *count it all joy when we fall into diverse temptations (James 1:2)* ... especially temptations to despair ... because He inhabits our praise.

I don't know about you, but I sure love the idea of Him inhabiting the very words that issue forth from my lips!

Discussion prompt: What is happening in your life right now that has you anxious, or worried, or fearful, or angry that you can commit to praising God for? You don't have to be able to see the *why* in the praise, you just have to be willing to praise Him for the ways He's going to *use* the situation.

Eight

And it came to pass, when Jesus had ended these sayings, the people were astonished at his doctrine. Matthew 7:28

A few years back, I was given a book written by a man with the absolute gift of storytelling. Not fictional stories, mind you. Real-life, actual and factual accounts from his own experience. I could not put the book down.

He captivated my attention and lassoed my heart with the way he strung words together to paint such a real, raw, and beautiful picture of God. He told of miraculous deliverances, times of persecution, faith struggles, and incredible victories in a way that inspired me in my own experience.

I wanted more. More Jesus.

Compare that with the way *we* often present Christianity. Sadly, we somehow make it seem like a stale loaf of bread that maybe even has begun to grow mold. Nobody wants it because we fail to present it with fresh passion, vigor, or enthusiasm.

In contrast is how far we swing the pendulum to the other side, trying to put forth a gospel that appeals to those who just aren't really interested. We humanize Christ, water down doctrine, falsify His testimony, and defer to adding in elements that draw a modern day society, even when they stand in contrast to the purity of Scripture.

Sure, it may bring people in through the doors when we take this approach, but it doesn't give them roots. It's building on the sand and the foundation gets washed away when the first big storm comes along. As quickly as they enter, they retreat. And often they do so without anyone going after them.

Satan has perverted the term *prophet* by raising so many who speak contrary to Scripture. They claim to have special enlightenment, or a word from God Himself, and then proceed to spew forth a message intended to destroy instead of build.

But the reality is, God spoke through people who recorded the messages He gave them in His Holy Word. Some prophesied of future events while others simply shared their testimony. And we are called to share ours. This is the surest and truest way to spread the gospel message.

The demoniac who encountered Jesus in the country of the Gadarenes (Mark 5:1-20) was so horrific that nobody could approach him. But when he became aware of Jesus' presence, he called out to Him, acknowledging His status as the Christ. The demons within him knew evil couldn't stand in the face of purity, and they begged to be allowed to enter the swine. We're told when the people came out to see what was happening, the man was sitting *clothed and in his right mind.*

When Jesus went to depart, the man begged to be allowed to go with Him. He'd found safety and deliverance in the One who came to restore fallen man to a loving Father. But Jesus instructed him that he needed to return home and tell everyone what had been done for him. The man obeyed and proclaimed throughout Decapolis about the Redeemer.

Do you think his story was dry, stale and without flavor? Absolutely not! He had a testimony to bear and as he bore it, the Scriptures say the people *marveled* (Mark 5:20).

We each have a testimony to bear, regardless of how long we've known Jesus. The demoniac was sent out as a missionary *immediately* after his conversion. He didn't sit in classes to learn how to preach or teach or evangelize. He didn't study all the latest methods or sift through options to find the best approach. He simply fell in love with the One who had come to rescue him, and out of love, he shared that story.

His experience was real and, as such, it was moving. Hearts were stirred. People were astonished at His doctrine. An unlearned man (in matters of Scripture) took the gospel to his people and captivated their hearts through the power of the Holy Spirit.

We can do the same. We should be *doing* the same.

If we know Jesus, we must share Him. It's the very pulse of our spiritual health.

Discussion prompt: Consider the ways in which you share Jesus. Do you do so with joy and light, or with sterness and intimidation? What can you learn from the demoniac's response to Christ's commission?

Nine

If ye abide in me, and my words abide in you, ye shall ask what ye will, and it shall be done unto you. John 15:7

I'd spent a quiet few hours with the Lord before the house began to stir. Those early morning hours refresh me like no others and, while it's often hard to drag myself out of bed, I'm always glad once I'm up.

Several years back, when we were still living in the US, I had developed the habit of walking circles around our home. At first it began as something symbolic but quickly turned into much more.

I had been sensing the slippery slope our family was on and knew that while we were professing Christians, living "decent" lives, we were on perilous ground because we hadn't securely connected our children with the Savior. I knew God was preparing me for "a new thing" He was going to do, if only I would allow Him. I had no idea what that meant, but I was ready for anything.

Or so I thought.

Weeks passed and I continued this discipline of walking and praying in the dawn of each morning. My experience with my Creator was deepening and places within me that had been dormant were beginning to stir.

About a month or so after this started, God made it clear He was asking us to sell everything, say goodbye to our friends and family, and move into the foreign mission field. Saying yes to that call felt strange, but even stranger was the lack of hesitation.

Fast forward a few years, and take a quick leap across the "pond" and you'd find us in Sukhothai, Thailand with 6 of our 8 children, plus 6 more God placed in our care since arriving. We were tired, a little weary, and a lot in over our heads.

So on this morning when I'd read from the Scriptures and circled the rice paddy praying, my heart was surrendered and submitted. I had enjoyed sweet communion and knew that God had bowed low to meet with me. As I walked back to the house to step into my role as mother, I asked the Spirit to go with me through the day.

As I walked through the door, I was met by a small brown boy whose face was disfigured by his obvious anger. A scene that plays out with far too much frequency for my liking, I sucked in a gulp of air and braced myself for the battle that was being waged almost before the sun had fully risen.

The sweetness of just moments before was still lingering over me, however, and by God's grace, I met the challenge with patience not natural to my carnal self. The situation quickly diffused and we all moved on. One incident after the other assailed my resolve to stay connected to the Spirit and each time I was present and abiding, which enabled me to avoid the downward spiral all too common in my several decades of mothering.

Around lunchtime, still at peace, I made my way with the others to the outdoor kitchen where we gather for meals. The blessing was prayed over the meal and plates began being served. And that's when the connection was broken.

Because after all morning of faithfully abiding, I let go.

My husband said something he thought was funny but I did not, and I felt myself stiffen in annoyance. He hadn't said anything grave or awful, just made a comment that I found abrasive rather than humorous. I'm a mother to many children which puts me at high-risk for slipping into playing the role of *his* mother instead of his wife. God had been showing me this tendency, and He called to me in that moment. It was, however, no longer convenient for me to listen.

I didn't snap at him or say anything at all for that matter. I did what I do most naturally when conflict arises and I became passive aggressive. I let him know with my body language and facial expressions that I was not pleased. I'm pretty sure it's safe to say that in those moments, I epitomize the contentious woman spoken of in Proverbs.

Not pretty and I'm not proud. But I *am* stubborn.

However, after a few minutes of seething quietly, I calmed enough to be ready and willing to listen to the gentle voice that was still calling for me. And as I did, the rebuke was swift, stern, but tender. How does God even do that? I heard Him speak straight into my heart telling me the behavior was in no way acceptable and that He wanted me to lay this burden of sin down at His feet and then get moving again.

I obeyed.

Things were made right, with both my husband and my God, and the fellowship I'd been enjoying with Him all morning was restored with only that small blip. Nighttime fell and I climbed into bed with a peace that only a day of walking with the Lord can bring.

I wish I could say more days were like this but I still buckle under too often. I cave to the temptation to let go, for even a second, and sometimes it takes me far too long to grab hold again.

But I'm learning that my best days come when I put every ounce of my energy into simply *abiding*. In fact, if I had a favorite word, I think that would be it.

Discussion prompt: Do you have regular personal worship? After a sweet season of communion with God, do you find it difficult to remain connected once you've stepped into the demands of the day? How can you safeguard against repeatedly falling into this pit?

Ten

And they overcame him by the blood of the Lamb, and by the word of their testimony; and they loved not their lives unto the death.
Revelation 12:11

We suddenly live in a world divided between mask-wearers and anti-maskers. Somehow something so small has become an issue maybe even more polarizing than vaccines used to be. Throw a new one of those (vaccines) into the mix and you have a recipe for disastrous terms of engagement and broken relationships.

Because the enemy is simply doing what the enemy does. He has literally one skill and it's destroying everything in his path. He doesn't care how he does it, or who he uses to accomplish his vile pleasure, just so long as he manages to crush as many people as possible in the process.

The casualties from his venom far outnumber the worldwide death toll from any virus.

Add to all this friction, the poison of fear. It's caused people to stop living. Some have literally checked out by taking their own lives, while others are barely hanging on. It started with the idea it would only be a few weeks, which turned into months, which has now begun rolling into its second year. Do you see it? Are you spotting his filthy fingerprints all over this calamity?

God's people are in hiding, afraid of what they can't see.

Churches are shuttered across the world. Pulpits are being silenced and, in some cases, chains and fences are being erected to prevent any defectors from gaining access to the buildings. Which brings us to the truth that the church is not a *building* and should stand even when the doors are closed. But that doesn't equal to God *wanting* them closed.

There are gray areas in even the Christian life. Areas where there isn't a one-size-fits-all answer. But the revealed will of God, as testified to in the Bible, is as black and white as it gets. And part of the revelation of His will comes from texts which forbid us to forsake the assembling of ourselves together, as the manner of some is. The passage goes on to say, *...but exhorting one another: **and so much the more, as ye see the day approaching.*** Hebrews 10:25

Practically speaking, this is commanding the doors be open, the place be consecrated to the Lord, and kept a safe space for war-battered pilgrims to find refuge. Can we truly justify loving our lives more than loving our neighbor?

Of course, the conversation can't stop there. Because the Spirit of God never intended to be confined to four walls. If the people can't come, or they won't come, or they want to come but haven't, *we* must go to *them*. We're the hands and feet of Jesus, pandemic or not.

If your health is frail and God is whispering that He's trusting you with a season of quiet, you can be sure He's still asking you to work to spread the gospel. To share your testimony. To teach and exhort others how to overcome by the blood of the Lamb.

There are countless ways to do it and being housebound for a time doesn't have to prevent you from walking in obedience. Write letters of encouragement to those whom God puts on your heart. Send groceries to someone who has lost their job and let them know a loving Father is looking after them. Call up a friend or family member you haven't heard from in awhile and tell them they've been on your mind and in your prayers. Start a prayer call where a group gathers using technology to pray together. Intensify your intercessory prayer experience by really building a list of names God gives you, faithfully presenting each person to Him. Grab your church directory and pray through it. Send your pastor a gift and encourage him that you're holding him, and his family, up in prayer. Many pastors are being faced with making decisions that could put them at odds with either their congregation or the law.

But also remember, God didn't create us to be hermits. It's unlikely that He'll call you to a life of solitude for any serious length of time. He has commissioned each of us to be torch-lighters, truthtellers, and gatekeepers who preserve the gospel message and keep it moving.

Bear your testimony before all you come in contact with. Your faith will increase as you are faithful, and someone else's life may depend on it.

During a time when so many are suffering from the world spinning off its axis, be salt and light. Do not be afraid.

Take courage because these words still hold true, even in a covid world: *Beloved, think it not strange concerning the fiery trail which is to try you, as though some strange thing happened unto you: But rejoice, inasmuch as ye are partakers of Christ's sufferings, that, when his glory shall be revealed ye may be glad also with exceeding joy. 1 Peter 4:12-13*

His word is faithful and His promise is true!

Discussion prompt: *No matter where you fall in the mask/vaccine debate, are you keeping your focus where it needs to be? Have you gotten caught up in the controversy or are you fastening your eyes on Jesus. Do you sense God asking you to reach out in ways or areas you've been neglecting?*

Eleven

For we wrestle not against flesh and blood, but against principalities, against powers, against the rulers of the darkness of this world, against spiritual wickedness in high places. Ephesians 6:12

We'd moved to the property only weeks before. The heat had given way slightly to lower temperatures that left the hint of chill hanging in the morning air. Yet, as I'd go out before the darkness had lifted, there was a heaviness I could neither explain nor escape.

Desperate to get back into my habit of walking outdoors while I prayed, rather than winding my way through the living room and kitchen until I was dizzy as I had in our previous house, I persisted in getting out there. I even asked Robbie to come with me.

It didn't matter. There was something, which I couldn't identify, that was disrupting the peace I'd been in the habit of experiencing. For a time I gave up and retreated back into the house, where I paced through whatever open space I could find. Still, there was an unexplainable presence and I couldn't settle into communion with God.

Weeks passed and strange things began happening. We'd hear voices in the night right beside our heads but we could see nobody with our eyes. There'd be scuffling or shuffling with no hint of who or what was causing it. Things would crash to the ground yet we could find nothing. Footsteps would pass by our windows with no visible body to explain who was there.

Oddly, we each heard these things and never spoke of them. I think we all believed ourselves to have overactive imaginations and so we'd inwardly scold ourselves for being silly and go back to sleep. Until the strangeness ramped up a bit more.

Because one afternoon Abigail came rushing over holding an extension cord from their room. It was charred and melted with no apparent cause. Upon inspection we found that the wood floor around it hadn't been harmed at all and there was no indication as to why it had happened. We pushed even that aside, knowing sometimes electrical malfunctions just happen, and we simply praised God that He'd prevented the situation from causing real harm.

But then one morning the electricity failed. Without enough juice to run even a small fan, we went to check the lights to see if they worked. They came on but were so dim you could barely be sure they were working at all. Robbie and Sneh (one of our Bible Workers) went looking for the cause. Finding nothing, they decided to return to one of the first places they had looked, just to double-check.

There they found the electrical wires smoking and melting right around the gated entrance to the property.

Determining the fix was a little beyond their abilities, they called someone to repair the problem and he had things up and running in fairly short order. We hoped the issue was behind us. Unfortunately, it wasn't.

That night Robbie heard a loud ripping sound and thought something had torn the screen on the window in our room. Getting up to check things out, he found all was intact and he went back to sleep. But the next afternoon we were all sitting together at the outdoor kitchen having lunch when the same sound cut through the air. Everyone got up to go check it out and found more electrical issues at the back of the house. As a result, we had to have our bedroom entirely re-wired.

Also, we were finally *really* starting to notice the red flags.

A few days later, we had all the kids in the car as we made the trip to deliver the ones who attend school at their respective buildings. Sitting at a traffic light after the last student had gotten out, I turned around and saw Quinn nearly in tears and asked him what was wrong.

"Everything hurts!" he shouted. I don't know why but, without hesitation, I asked Robbie to drive directly to the hospital. And though he'd typically argue such a sudden and seemingly irrational idea, he did exactly that. A short time later we had a pneumonia diagnosis. But that was only the beginning of a battle for restoration of health with this previously healthy child.

As I paced in the parking lot on that sunny morning, one thing became clear: the enemy wasn't tossing sidelong darts at us anymore. Instead, he was making a near-frontal attack. I prayed a desperate prayer, which I can only be grateful was interpreted by the Holy Spirit, and then I asked a few friends to start praying with us.

From that day on, the strange occurrences around the property ceased. All of it. We were delivered from the evil presence that was tormenting us day and night and peace settled back over the place. Prayer … intercessory prayer … delivered us, I'm convinced of it. God heard the cries of our friends and He answered.

So often when we encounter the enemy, we try to reason the chaos away as just something that happens. But the truth is, when he gets scared his territory is being encroached on, Satan flies into a rage and attacks with fury. We blame circumstances, or coincidence, or happen-chance. We blame each other. We look for a human way to reason what we're up against and, far too often, relationships are broken as a result.

We do everything *except* remember that we wrestle not against flesh and blood, which causes us to fail to see the real culprit behind the struggle. Our eyes are blind to the principalities and powers that are ruling this dark world, so far as they're granted permission.

We need to keep our eyes on the light so that, when it gets

dimmed, we can recognize right away who is the source of the darkness.

Discussion prompt: What are some situations where you circled around to blaming situations or people for that which was a full-on attack of the enemy?

Twelve

Beloved, think it not strange concerning the fiery trial which is to try you, as though some strange thing happened unto you: But rejoice, inasmuch as ye are partakers of Christ's sufferings; that, when his glory shall be revealed, ye may be glad also with exceeding joy.
1 Peter 4:12-13

This text became a life verse for me several months into the process of preparing to leave the United States for Thailand. We knew He had called and, while we certainly experienced moments of not wanting to go, we never seriously doubted what He was asking. But clearly the adversary knew we were stagnating where we were and that, if we stayed, we'd only grow worse.

So he did everything he could to keep us from going.

The moment our house went on the market, we began having showings. It was located in an area on top of a mountain where properties had been known to sit for years without selling. There we were, listing ours less than 5 months from when we planned to leave the country. From a human perspective, it didn't look good.

The first people who looked at it made an offer, but then we never heard a peep out of them or their realtor. Our agent told us she'd rarely ever had someone just totally fall off the radar like that, but there we were with a buyerless offer. Starting over, we moved forward and, in relatively short order, we had another offer. This time it went under official contract and remained there for 2 weeks until the buyer suddenly pulled out.

Back to square one with the sands in the hourglass rapidly slipping away. But then, just when we were beginning to doubt, not the calling but the timing, another offer came. The contract was signed, inspections were completed, and the required repairs and upgrades were made.

We were in several thousand dollars pretty quickly with the type of loan they were getting and each day seemed to bring new requests. More money went out and more problems creeped up. The whole thing seemed to be on very shaky ground but Robbie knew he had to give notice to his work. So with a million reasons to wait, and only the instruction we believed we'd gotten from God to proceed, he let them know he'd be leaving. They asked him to be very sure before making his notice official, and he told them he was.

Then the thousands of dollars for the tickets had to be purchased without proof that the house would even make it to closing. Each day brought more evidence that it wasn't likely to close. Again, we had only the still, small voice of God leading us forward into territory that seemed unwise to just about everyone around us. The roughly $5000 purchase was made and we began to pack.

No sooner did those suitcases begin to fill than we got word the buyers had lost their loan. We were less than a week from closing. Thankfully, we had good friends around us who encouraged us to look back on how God had led over the months leading up to that day, and they asked us to keep trusting.

The buyers found a new lender, but the loan wouldn't close before we left the country. It was a risk but what in life, that's worth pursuing, isn't?

We applied for our visas, determined not to be delayed by anything but the will of God. We moved out of our house, the buyers took early occupancy because they had nowhere else to go, and we stayed at the AirBnB of our friends. Suddenly, we were to the Sunday before our Wednesday flight and we still had no visas. But more than that, we had no passports since the visa applications had required they be sent along. More waiting, more trusting, more praying.

Farewell parties were thrown and we attended not knowing if we were actually leaving. It felt strange and a few well-intentioned people even suggested that if God was truly leading, we wouldn't be encountering so much difficulty.

We were tempted to agree until we checked ourselves before God and were assured it wasn't so.

On Monday, Robbie made the trip to the Embassy in Washington, DC to see what he could find out about our visas. What he learned wasn't what we'd been hoping; they hadn't even begun processing them. Out of time, he was told he could take them and we could enter the country on tourist visas, though we'd be counselled not to since the sheer number of our group was likely to raise some eyebrows. There was the chance we'd find ourselves on the outside looking in. But there was no choice.

Two days later we were at the airport, winding our way to the gate wondering for all the world if we'd lost our minds. We had, of course, but only so we could be renewed in the *spirit* of our minds. (Ephesians 4:23)

A new journey had begun and it's been a wild one. We've found that the closer we press into God, the more struggle we find ourselves up against, but also the greater testimony of deliverance we have to share.

It's been a trade-off … the known and comfortable for a life of the unknown where our faith is tested, our patience is threatened, our perseverance is challenged, and our courage is battered.

But always, without fail, God dips low and shows us afresh that the fiery trials are there to purify us and that, one day, we will *be glad also with exceeding joy* as we stand face to face in His presence.

If only we will allow Him to cover us with His feathers, so we can find safety under His gentle wings. (Paraphrased from

Psalm 91:7)

Discussion prompt: Can you think of a time where you believed God had given you instructions only to find yourself up against one obstacle after the other? How did you respond?

Thirteen

Remember ye not the former things, neither consider the things of old. Behold, I will do a new thing; now it shall spring forth; shall ye not know it? I will even make a way in the wilderness, and rivers in the desert. Isaiah 43:18-19

One of my older boys found himself tired and confused and completely hooked on drugs. I could see the signs of him slipping away and was doing all I knew how in order to go after him.

Nothing would stay his spiral out of control. He didn't want the help being offered him. I was beside myself and this was all happening as God was preparing us to leave the country.

There I was, torn between two worlds, and knowing I could choose only the one to which God was directing. But I couldn't silence the screaming of my heart. How could I abandon my beloved child, in his darkest hours, to go attempt to help others. Clearly I had nothing to offer or I wouldn't be in this situation to begin with. What kind of fraud leaves a son, with a potentially mortal wound, to fend for himself?

It was the struggle of a lifetime and I very nearly lost the strength to surrender to God's will various times over the months leading to our departure.

But even as I watched him slip further away, God was faithful to show me clear evidence that He had him. That the time had come to release him from my care into His. My position in my son's life was the same, but my role was now different.

After leaving America, I watched from afar as he sunk deeper, and despair would at times threaten to overtake me. I'd spend fitful nights, getting little sleep, before spending early mornings pleading for him to be helped. I prayed for God to allow *anything*, no matter how painful it was to walk through, if only He'd position Nik for surrender.

Anything.

One morning, as I paced while praying, a strange peace came over me. I was confused because all I could see was turmoil. Why the sudden peace? But then today's verse came to my mind and I knew God was assuring me He was making a way for my child. A way of escape. He'd prepared a rescue.

I could share a thousand details, but because this is his story to tell (or not tell) one day, I won't. {I did get his permission to share this portion of it here} But the following months brought him to a new low, and I struggled to believe there was hope. Yet, in the recesses of my mind, I knew what God had whispered to me that morning weeks before.

He was doing a new thing. Blazing a way through the wilderness of addiction and a river through the desert of despair. I couldn't see it but I could make the choice to believe it.

With trembling legs, I chose to trust. And as soon as I did, the bottom seemingly dropped out. Again and again, God had to direct my mind back to the promise of that Scripture. The way I was interpreting the situation was that his life was crumbling before my eyes. But God kept insisting to my heart that *now it shall spring forth*!

We're so unaccustomed to using spiritual eyesight because we're conditioned to see only through finite vision. As such, we see through a glass dimly and the picture is grossly incomplete

Time passed, and any real progress seemed to ebb and flow right along with clear regression. Until the call came. The call asking if he could come to Thailand.

Little did he know I'd been praying for this very thing since before we'd left America. I knew my adult sons weren't experiencing the call to this place like we were, but I also knew, deep within me, that God was impressing me to ask for the way to open *for this specific son* to come, at least for a season.

He'd gently remind me there was no magic in the place and not to pin my hopes on seeing outward change while he was here. Perhaps it would take returning home for the impact of his experience to hit him. I didn't know and God didn't offer even a hint.

We picked him up from the airport, after miraculous intervention to get him here in the midst of a covid-controlled world, and he was smiling but fidgety. I braced myself for the worst, believing it would come. I was smart enough to know it could get ugly.

But it hasn't. Conversations have been had. Conflict has been worked through. Differences have been discussed. Incredible ground has been gained.

Strings have been tied tighter rather than coming unloosed.

It's been a scary experience trusting God with my young men while the enemy works to convince me I've abandoned my post. And I don't pretend that I know how this story will end.

Free will is a gift that Satan works to twist into a curse. But always my fragile mind is reminded that God *will* do His part and He doesn't need *me* in the way. I'm watching new promise unfold and I believe the end will be far better than the beginning.

Because the former things have passed away and the path ahead is alight with hope. *Shall ye not know it?*

Discussion prompt: Is there someone you've been praying for where you've been tempted to despair? Is there a situation in your own life that feels as though you'll never be able to break free? How does this verse speak to you?

Fourteen

No man can enter into a strong man's house, and spoil his goods, except he will first bind the strong man; and then he will spoil his house. Mark 3:27

It's arguable depending through which theological lens you look, but it *could* be said the devil has been careful to build his fortress on somewhat solid ground. He's thought things through, strategically planned, and fully committed to his course of evil. He's skilfully trained his vile cohorts, rather than sending them willy nilly into the world.

Of course, we know the foundation is cracked because it was constructed in intentional opposition to the law and character of God. But that doesn't negate the fact that God has allowed him to retain strength and dominion over his would-be followers.

The people of Thailand are largely Buddhist, though there is also Muslim and Hindu presence, along with a *very* small smattering of Christianity. And the Thai people, in a general sense, have adopted a mix of these religions.

It's not uncommon to find a regular attendee of a Christian church wearing an amulet or pendent around their neck. They are very aware of, and fearful about, the spirit world and so even when they embrace Christianity, it's often an add-on instead of a replacement.

I've been so confused and perplexed by this, but then God began showing me what I've been missing.

How often do we learn something new about God … believe it, accept it, and adopt it … without considering what it actually entails? We make a profession *without an understanding,* and that never works.

It's sort of like being convicted going to a movie theatre to watch the latest blockbuster is bad, but that watching it when it's released on DVD is fine. Something about watching from the confines of your home sanctifies the evil message within the movie, right?

Not even a little.

And so you have a well-meaning individual, trying to make a reform to adopt their new beliefs, without grasping the actual purpose.

A house that's not swept clean will simply accumulate more dust. And that's what we tend to do when we begin to accept the gospel message. We embrace the parts of it we're comfortable with, while rejecting the ones that rub, even as we cling to the aspects of our "old" beliefs we don't feel ready to part with. We aren't all in or all out and Satan has a jolly good time while he has us pinned somewhere in the middle.

But it says in Luke 16:13 that *No servant can serve two masters: for either he will hate the one, and love the other; or else he will hold to the one, and despise the other. Ye cannot serve God and mammon.* It may seem like it's working for awhile but it will always, *always* fail.

The first thing to do is offer yourself before God, accepting His work of purging. He must be able to strip you of idols, vices, besetting sins, and false teachings. It's a process that almost never happens at once, but rather is an exercise whereby you must continually re-surrender to the work He's doing. If you buy into the lie that you have to fix yourself first and *then* come to Him, you'll never come. The strong man's house will always stand in the way.

But once the Holy Spirit is invited in, He can begin to dismantle that which the strong man had built, until the entire structure is knocked down and the whole house is spoiled. As long as *God* is then allowed to rebuild and fill the cracks and corners, you'll remain safe from the first master returning to take up residence as a squatter.

I'm learning these precious Thai people are no different than us. Their masters may look a little different because I didn't come across too many spirit houses as I walked through my American neighborhoods. And I didn't encounter too many people making intricately woven flowers to sell to people at traffic lights because the buyers believe somehow the purchase keeps them just a little bit safer.

But we erect and imagine our own masters, and they're equally as pervasive and deceptive.

We need to stop everything, right where we are, and give God permission to pull down whatever strongholds are still standing between us and Him. Because it's not until we do, that He can truly enter into our hearts in the fullness He intends.

Discussion prompt: What ways have you embraced the gospel message, without submitting to God, as He's asked you to forsake those things which stand contrary to His character? What do you want to do about it?

Fifteen

And be not conformed to this world: but be ye transformed by the renewing of your mind, that ye may prove what is that good, and acceptable, and perfect, will of God. Romans 12:2

If the world today isn't just flat out confused, I don't know what it is.

We have mastered the art of breaking rules while simultaneously making new ones. We say we don't like the confines of society, and yet we attempt to confine others to *our* beliefs.

We have causes and soapboxes and social media rants and cryptic manifestos. We have strong opinions and even stronger disdain for those who dissent. We want purpose but we completely miss the point in our quest to find it.

And this has become the norm.

Fewer and fewer Daniels can be found. Scarcer and more rare are those who will stand for truth, even when it's unfavorably received. In a society that can shut you down, or cut you off in an instant, we prefer to just fit in.

A young man named, Ryan, dared to defy his friends. He'd encountered Christ casually a few years ago but the death of his father nearly took him out.

Because in his grief, he'd fallen almost beyond reach and yet the Father's arm was not shortened nor was His ear deaf to the hurting man's cry.

A older gentleman named, Dave, found Ryan just off the street one night, as snow fell in huge flakes all around him. He had no coat and only tennis shoes protecting his feet. He was cold but didn't notice. He'd run with the wrong crowd so long, his body was nearly numb to the usual warning signs of physical distress. And so he walked aimlessly up the street, not noticing the people who were surely shooting sidelong glances his way.

The light from a gas station apparently caught his eye and his feet began moving in its direction. Though he was unaware of his need, something inside him must have been screaming for warmth.

Closing in on the place, he headed for the door despite the fact that he had no plan for what he would do inside. But Dave had been watching. He'd seen the empty look in his eyes and he recognized a younger version of himself as the freezing man moved toward the station.

Breathing a quiet prayer, Dave moved into position between

the young man and the door. As the two men's eyes met, they said nothing. Dave reached down, slipped off his boots and handed them to Ryan, still saying nothing.

Snapping slowly out of his stupor, the young man furrowed his brow as Dave stood there in his socks, with boots extended. They maintained eye contact for a moment until Dave broke the silence and said simply, "I've been where you are. All it took was knowing someone cared."

Dave handed him a card with his number and walked back to his car, while little balls of snow began clinging to his socks.

Ryan stood, motionless, watching him walk away. He wasn't sure whether the guy was crazy, psychic, or just a do-gooder. But there was a quickening within him as he stood there, boots in hand, feeling seen.

That was a turning point in Ryan's life and while he didn't want to abandon the people who'd been his friends for years, as he came to know Christ he knew he needed to be careful of the company he kept. So he started inviting them to join him at public events where he wouldn't be tempted to slip into old ways. He endured a lot of teasing and jokes as the guys called him things like *Old Man* and *St. Ryan*. But the fullness with which he embraced the truth, and with Dave as a faithful mentor, the chains that had held him were broken.

He didn't care what anyone said about him, so long as he was right with God. A few of his old friends dismissed him, but Ryan was so patient that others began to be interested in the

One who had worked the change in his life. Through him they saw a glimpse of hope for something better, and they wanted what he'd found.

The world doesn't need a bunch of conformists, squeezing into the same box of causes as everyone else. The world needs people of courage, willing stand alone if necessary, unfazed by not fitting in.

One life, surrendered to *God's* cause, will do more good for humanity than all the Christless soapbox-ers could ever hope to do!

Discussion prompt: Have you ever been a Ryan? What about a Dave?

Sixteen

*And he said, Go forth, and stand upon the mount before the Lord.
And, behold, the Lord passed by, and a great and strong wind rent
the mountains, and brake in pieces the rocks before the Lord; but the
Lord was not in the wind: and after the wind an earthquake; but the
Lord was not in the earthquake: And after the earthquake a fire;
but the Lord was not in the fire: and after the fire a still small voice.
1 Kings 19:11-12*

When I was a child, we spent some time living with my grandparents. It was a tiny, two-bedroom, one bathroom apartment and we squeezed 8 of us in there. My memories are cozy, although those who were adults at the time likely don't have such warm and fuzzy feelings looking back.

My Pap liked things orderly and was very routine driven. His clothes were always just so, his hair always in place. He'd walk in the apartment, remove his shoes, and put on his slippers. When he ate ice cream, he'd stir it until it was like soft serve but eat it before it was soup.

He had a method for just about everything.

One of my responsibilities was dusting and that involved straightening the bookshelves holding my Pap's collection of books. He liked the books pushed all the way to the front edge of the shelves with everything lined up evenly. I seem to remember not enjoying the job as child, but I did love my Pap and so I don't think I complained much.

Among those books was a large, illustrated Bible. He and my Gram weren't church-goers at the time, but both were believers and well-studied. I'd pull the beautiful book from the shelf and run my hand over the soft cover and then flip through the pages. I knew nothing of God but something in that book just compelled me to hold it.

It was an especially difficult time in my young life as my dad had been arrested and jailed. I've always been blessed with family who loved me, and the absence of my father was painful. I'd spend nights crying myself to sleep imagining him scared and alone in a prison cell. But God had seen to it that my brothers and I were always surrounded by love and that little apartment is where I caught my first glimpses of Jesus.

From the picture on the wall depicting the Last Supper, to the casual chats over Friday night pizza, to that big Bible that so captivated me, I was hooked.

I didn't know Him, or how to serve Him, but something deep inside me wanted to.

One day I took a piece of paper and, while I don't remember what it was, I wrote something on it asking God to do something to show me He was real. I can't be sure because my memory is a little foggy, but I'm almost positive I asked Him to either *take* the paper or write back to me on it.

In any case, I do remember that what I asked for on that scrap of paper wasn't answered. Or so I thought.

Because what I was really asking was for some kind of proof that He was real, and interested, and that He cared for even a straggly-haired little girl with an overbite and a too-loud laugh. What I didn't understand until decades later was that He did, in fact, answer my request.

He showed me in a thousand different ways that He loved me. He took care of my family countless times when things seemed hopeless. He walked me through high school, and though I made many decisions I desperately regret, He always kept alive within me a *desire* to hold to a high moral standard. He gave me a pitying heart for the underdog and I hated anyone to be left out. I was an absolute mess at the exact same time as I was being redeemed by a God I still really didn't know beyond trite prayers before drifting off to sleep at night.

But what really stands out to me is that I have no miraculous, transformative conversion experience to share. I didn't hit a low in my life and suddenly have my eyes opened wide to the Savior. There was no near-death incident that brought me to His feet. No stranger off the street walked up with a message from God that changed me forever.

My experience was slow and steady. It was the gentle influence of grandparents, who I don't even share blood with, that first opened the way for me to know Jesus.

We like the big stories and most of us wish we had one. But the truth is, God often speaks in a loving whisper to the heart, and leads with a tender hand. No fireworks or earthquakes but a still small voice that calls to us so long as we have breath.

And amen.

Discussion prompt: What is your story? How did you find Jesus and with whom can you share that testimony?

Seventeen

Sow to yourselves in righteousness, reap in mercy; break up your fallow ground: for it is time to seek the Lord, till he come and rain righteousness upon you.
Isaiah 30:21

I'd been sensing something just wasn't right. To those on the outside looking in, things appeared to be moving quickly. Yet we knew God was holding back the fullness of His blessing.

At first, I was tempted to believe we were just getting ahead of His timing and there was a purpose in the wait. I, like so many others, saw a bump in the plan and assumed we were still on track, but just needed a little pause while the will of God caught up. Basically, I was choosing to believe the hold-up wasn't us, it was Him.

And to be fair, that does happen. There are countless legitimate times God asks us to wait until the timing for a thing is just right, for reasons we can't see. But as I was walking, and reviewing memory verses, I fell under sudden, but *strong,* conviction that wasn't the case here.

God clearly began taking me through a reasoning process, and making it evident that His plan was being held up by *us*. I was honestly a little shocked and almost embarrassed. Here we were thinking things were going well and suddenly God was saying, "There's sin in the camp!"

I spent more than an hour that morning asking Him what to do. He kept taking my mind back to the story of Achan in Joshua 7. With the fall of Jericho still fresh, the Israelites had sent a few hundred men up to fight the Amorites, expecting an easy victory. Only they were defeated instead. Covering his head with dust, Joshua fell on his face before the Lord. Instead of leaving him there, God commanded him to get up and then He informed the desperate man that Israel had sinned.

One man, and one sin, had hindered the blessing and protection of God. One man, and one sin, had killed 36 men that day. One man, and one sin, was preventing God's will from being accomplished on behalf of His chosen people.

Hard to fathom, right? Yet I knew that morning, with absolute certainty, that God was telling me something similar. Only I was falling under the conviction it was more than one sin, and more than one man (or woman) committing them.

God was breaking up the fallow ground of my heart and informing me it was time to get serious and truly seek the Lord. It was time to sanctify ourselves, no longer comfortable being "good enough", and consecrate ourselves before Him. He convicted my mind, over and again, that it was only then He'd be able to pour out His intended blessing and accomplish His will, enabling the work here to move forward.

I'm slow and stubborn but I'm not dumb. I didn't hesitate. I returned to the house and told Robbie what God had shown me. And my humble husband took it all in and said, "Well, let's search ourselves then."

A day passed and God spoke loud enough for me to hear again, instructing that our older girls needed to be apart of this. And so we talked with them and they received the instructions well. A plan was made and a time of consecration was enacted.

We agreed to each ask God to search us, revealing that which was standing between us and Him. We'd write down what He revealed and bring the paper to a group meeting. What was written on each person's paper wouldn't be made known to the others, but we'd be bringing a copy because, after a season of prayer and confession, we'd be taking them out back to burn.

Symbolic of how we're letting those things go.

I have no idea how the days ahead will unfold but I do know one thing for certain: when God says there's sin in the camp, there is. No amount of hiding from it, or pretending, will undo that fact.

If we truly want His Spirit to come and rest upon us, we need to repent, sow in righteousness, reap in mercy, and seek the Lord. It's then that He'll rain righteousness upon us.

It's only then.

Discussion prompt: Is there sin in your camp? Are you willing to ask God to reveal it to you and then repent of it?

Eighteen

And Jesus said unto him, No man, having put his hand to the plough, and looking back, is fit for the kingdom of God. Luke 9:62

Before coming to the mission field, the president of our foundation shared a message through email that his high school daughter had presented at her school. In it was a story that has stuck with me ever since. I don't remember every detail perfectly, but the lesson is ingrained in my mind.

A man had been called to serve in a foreign land. He had a wife and several small sons and apparently they had begun making plans to follow the call. Somewhere along the way, however, the man learned the area was inhabited by various types of venomous snakes. From a rational, practical, responsible, *human* perspective, taking his family into a place of such danger just didn't make sense.

And so he didn't.

He and his wife chose to stay and begin a ministry in the United

States. Safer, but still working for God, it seemed like the perfect compromise. But was it? Because as the story continued, it told of how the boys had been playing outdoors and one of them had been bitten by, you guessed it, a venomous snake.

In their rush to get him help, the other boy was run over by their vehicle. In one day, his two sons were killed, and it all happened in the security of their "safe" ministry that wasn't what God had called them to do.

To be certain, I don't believe God to be vengeful and so if you take a story like that at face value, you might decide He is. Some poor family was trying to serve Him while simultaneously protecting their little ones and because they didn't follow the exact specifications, tragedy befell them. Seems a bit harsh if you leave it right there.

But in the book of Psalms, chapter 91, we find the prescription for safety. It says:

*He that **dwelleth in the secret place** of the most High shall abide under the **shadow of the Almighty**. I will say of the Lord, He is my **refuge and my fortress:** my God; in him will I trust. Surely he shall deliver thee from the **snare of the fowler**, and from the noisome pestilence. **He shall cover thee with his feathers**, and under his wings shalt thou trust: his truth shall be thy shield and buckler. **Thou shalt not be afraid for the terror by night; nor for the arrow that flieth by day;** Nor for the pestilence that walketh in darkness; nor for the destruction that wasteth at noonday. A thousand shall fall at thy side, and ten thousand at thy right hand; **but it shall not come nigh thee.** (vs. 1-7)*

No amount of human reasoning can keep us safer, or more secure, than going where God leads. It doesn't matter if we don't *want* to be there, or we don't want to *stay* there, or we'd rather serve Him *here*, or it suits us better to *wait* until the kids are older.

We aren't ever told about Abraham sitting down having a chat with Sarah, covering the pros and cons of going to a place they did not know, for a reason they did not understand, for a length of time they had not been told. And once they'd gone, there's no accounting of discussions where they considered if they wanted to return instead of proceed.

God had spoken and they obeyed. Because His word, and His will, trump everything.

All the time, people say things like, *I'm not cut out for that* or *It just wouldn't suit my lifestyle* or *If God wanted me to do that He'd have created me to **want** to do it.*

But, no!

This life is a vapor and every single converted Christian is called to lay theirs down on the altar and pick up the cross God has for them. No excuses, no exemptions.

Putting your hand to the plough, and then turning back, is arguably more dangerous than not having put your hand to the plough at all. It shouldn't even be an option.

Discussion prompt: Is there something God has asked of you that you've been shrinking from because it doesn't match your desires? Or perhaps there's something you've obeyed Him in but have since grown weary? What is He saying to you in response?

Nineteen

So likewise, whosoever he be of you that forsaketh not all that he hath, he cannot be my disciple. Salt is good: but if the salt have lost his savour, wherewith shall it be seasoned? Luke 13:33-34

Sacrifice. How little we truly understand it.

We offer from our abundance and comfort ourselves it's enough. We serve where we want to, and take pride in our efforts. We give until it feels good, instead of until it hurts.

Almost instantly upon arriving in Thailand the reality of what we'd done smacked us in the face. We were a world away from the rest of our family (including three of our boys), all of our friends, the foods we had loved, and everything we had known. The whole idea had suddenly lost its appeal.

Our minds were consumed with going back. Everything in us was screaming RETREAT!

Because when the call to our hearts had first come, it had been scary but exciting. It was an answer to a prayer we didn't realize we'd prayed, and it *felt good* to be noticed by God. We felt important and like something big was ahead. God would use us for great things and we might even leave a mark on the world.

I'm almost certain we each probably thought these things, though none of us were brave enough to admit it. Our foolish hearts were filled with pride, even as God was beginning to purge us.

The months following the call took sacrifice, in the best way we understood it, as we sold what we had and whittled our lives down to what could fit in our bags, or the few boxes we were leaving behind.

People wished us well, assured us they were praying, and entrusted us with money we didn't ask for. It *felt good* to be doing something so notable. And as we said our goodbyes and the tears wouldn't stop, it was a little more real but it still *felt* pretty good. We'd visit soon and tell them all about the great things God was using us to accomplish.

The salt quickly lost its savor, however.

Our church family had sent us with cards and a journal in which they'd written us little notes. Those first days in Chiang Mai we'd try to read one each time we gathered for family worship, but our throats would close and the tears would come, making it difficult to read aloud. The pain of separation, the reality of all that had been left, was just too great. God seemed to be asking the impossible and it just didn't seem fair.

There was nobody around to even notice our struggle or applaud us for our perseverance. So we sat in our despair, alone and uncelebrated.

Let me just tell you something that doesn't feel good: admitting all this. Writing it down for every critical eye to see.

As the weeks turned into months, the sun dipped behind a cloud of covid. Our visit home was cancelled because the world stopped turning, and now it was the *nations* calling for retreat. My heart ached because the hope of seeing my boys fell flat and I was struggling with anger over having to give them up against my will. It no longer felt good. The cost was too great and I wanted out. I was willing to give of myself, but not this. Not them.

But because God is patient and loving and kind, He walked alongside me through my crisis. He talked me down and held me up. He loved me too well to bring me so far only to have me run away. And so He stayed the course, tenderly teaching me to do the same.

Over a year and a half in, I'm fully settled here. While God recently brought one of our older boys over, we'll likely have crossed the two year mark before I see the others. And in a world suddenly controlled by the circulation of a virus, it *could* be never.

I've learned, albeit slowly, that while my heart sometimes takes a beating, I cannot be His disciple unless I "forsake all" and submit my life, and theirs, into His hands. I can't surrender control while holding onto it.

I want nothing more than to be salt that hasn't lost its savor.

Discussion prompt: What are you holding back? Do you have unintentional limits with God where you silently scream, "This far and no farther!"?

Twenty

Finally, brethren, pray for us, that the word of the Lord may have free course, and be glorified, even as it is with you. 2 Thessalonians 3:1

I first took notice of this verse in the New King James Version and I love the wording there; *that the word of the Lord may run swiftly and be glorified.* How beautiful is that word picture?

Not quite a week ago, the husband of a friend from our previous village called me. I picked up the phone expecting him to be asking about English classes for his daughter, and quickly learned I couldn't have been more wrong. After greeting me and inquiring as to how we were doing, he informed me his 5 year old son had died suddenly the day before.

I was literally and utterly and completely speechless.

This little boy, Archie, had struggled to regain his health after something had gone awry with his kidneys. When we met them he was bloated to at least twice his normal size and walking was extremely difficult for him. They spent months traveling to and from Bangkok where they met with specialists attempting to get him well. And before we moved from that village, he was doing amazing! His swelling had subsided and he could be seen playing outside and laughing like a normal, healthy child.

But on that fateful day, my kids had been visiting with another of the neighbor boys back in that village. They saw Archie swimming in his kiddie pool. Shortly thereafter, he got in the car with his dad to take a road trip about an hour away. At some point, they stopped for food and then ate while driving along. Only Archie choked on a fish ball and his dad couldn't get it loose.

He rushed him to the hospital where they managed to get it out, but Archie had been without oxygen and his heart had stopped. They got it going again but it was quickly determined he had no brain activity. The shocked parents were faced with the reality of someday taking their child home to never again walk or play or laugh, but the next morning his heart gave up. The father called to tell us and spoke in such detached frankness that it was almost alarming.

Accompanied by our monk friend, Ram, we went to the Buddhist temple for the funeral. And the hopelessness was almost overwhelming. Ram explained to us what the Buddhist religion teaches happens upon death and, according to this teaching, the family has absolutely zero hope of ever seeing him again.

When it ended and we went to leave, I squeezed the arm of my friend, who'd shown no emotion the whole evening, and she dropped into the seat beside me. There were no words; it was simply a moment of sitting with her in her grief. As I stood to go, the look in her eyes was pleading, almost desperate. It was like she knew I know what *she* needs to know.

I didn't have the vocabulary to share it and I've never been more angry at my slow grasp of the Thai language. But God has since comforted me that He's told us not to worry about what we'll say when brought before kings or courts, because He'll be the one to supply the words. I believe it'll be the same with this family. When the time is right and their ears aren't clouded by grief, He'll present the opportunity and provide the words. Perhaps if I thought I had them, I'd have spoken them out of turn.

But that little boy slipping away so suddenly, leaving his unprepared parents behind, made me realize with new force how difficult it must be for God to look the world over and see so many who've had no chance to embrace the gospel.

We were reminded at a missionary retreat several months ago, that it's not our responsibility to *win* souls for Christ. And our success can't be gauged by how many respond to the message we share. Success in ministry is putting the gospel in front of as many people as possible, so they have the *opportunity* to make a decision to accept Jesus.

That's it. Friendship evangelism. Interest in the lives of others. Lifting the burdens of the downtrodden. It's to be a lifestyle, not a side gig. Because people are dying without knowing Him and that should break us.

The very fact that it doesn't should be alarming, causing us to repent of our stony hearts and compelling us to ask for hearts like Jesus'.

We're watching time wind down, faster all the time. The word of the Lord must be allowed to run swiftly, that He might be glorified, and as many as possible might be saved.

Discussion prompt: Does it bother you to know there are people dying without ever hearing the name of Jesus? Does your response, or lack thereof, concern you?

Twenty-one

The words of a man's mouth are as deep waters, and the wellspring of wisdom as a flowing brook. Proverbs 18:4

It was several decades ago but I remember it the same as if it had just happened last week. We were at a church and stayed afterwards for the potluck fellowship meal. We walked to the dining area and found seats surrounded by friends, enjoying edifying conversation. With several small children, I was kept busy being sure they were appropriately occupied until the prayer had been said and the line began to form at the tables laden with a variety of steamy dishes.

With a child on my hip and one at each side, I walked toward the line to get plates. As I neared the tables, however, I heard the loud voices of two ladies who'd made it there ahead of me.

They were apparently known for their temperance and health emphasis and were leaders in the church, directing others to healthier lifestyles. But what I heard coming from their lips that day seemed so contrary to the character of the God I was slowly coming to know.

Because they were holding near empty plates, having made their way about halfway through the lineup of dishes. And they were pointing fingers at many of the selections and saying things like, "Well, that's not fit for food!" and "That wouldn't be safe for even my *dog*." and "My family won't be touching *that*!". I was so embarrassed for the ladies around who had been the ones to bring the offending entrees.

My heart hurt and I felt my appetite slip away.

I wasn't so young, or so new to mothering, that I didn't understand the importance of care when it comes to what we put into our bodies. But it seemed contradictory to me, to so carelessly crush someone's spirit while preaching about health.

I went through the line, probably making choices I wouldn't have otherwise, and then proceeded to thank the women who had taken the time to make those dishes. I don't know that my approach was the correct one, but everything in me was desperate to try to bandage the wounds the unkind words had inflicted.

I've seen this type of thing play out so many times over the course of the many years since that day. Times where I just could not understand the cruelty with which a person could share *even truth* without regard for the feelings of another.

Obviously, there's the extreme that swings the other direction where we try so hard not to offend *people* that we offend *God*. I'm not advocating for that, either.

But surely the Spirit must attend our words or, true or not, they'll often do more damage than good. Which brings my mind to another occasion that happened at least 5 years after the first. A time that has also stuck in my mind, but for a very different reason.

It was a weekday evening and I was at church, sitting at a table with a group of ladies. Plans were being laid for an event where food would be served. Some of the women were more "liberal" in their dietary approach while one or two of them was far more "conservative". A list was being made about who would be bringing what, and some of the items mentioned didn't exactly sit well with one of the ladies. But rather than assert herself as an authority over all things diet and health, she humbly asked if the others might be interested in trying some new recipes.

The recipes went along with a recent seminar the church had offered to the public about reversing heart disease through diet and lifestyle. She framed her suggestion as a way to continue that discussion with people who had attended, since several would likely attend the upcoming one, as well. And because she was so meek and cautious with the feelings of the others, not a single woman present resisted her idea.

A menu was created that would be both nourishing and tasty, continuity in the message being presented to the public would be maintained, and a number of the women walked away with new recipes to try out. Everyone was happy, nobody felt judged, and no spirits had been crushed in the process.

I thought it was such a beautiful contrast to my experience

those years before and I learned a lesson that day. Both times the women were calling people to a higher, *or more carefully considered*, standard of eating. But the first was done by spewing information and passing harsh judgment. The second, however, was done by appealing to the natural desire to learn something new, while being mindful that each person is at a different place in their journey.

What a difference our words can, and do, make.

But it's important to remember that words *spoken* begin as words *thought*. Philippians 4:8 has this to say about those thoughts ... *Finally, brethren, whatsoever things are true, whatsoever things are honest, whatsoever things are just, whatsoever things are pure, whatsoever things are lovely, whatsoever things are of good report; if there be any virtue, and if there be any praise, think on these things.*

Filtering our thoughts will enable the Holy Spirit to cause what comes forth from our lips to be a *wellspring of wisdom as a flowing brook.*

All I can say is, sign me up!

Discussion prompt: Is talking without thinking something you struggle with? Do you battle the thoughts taking flight in your mind? If so, what is God calling you to do about it?

Twenty-two

Be careful for nothing; but in every thing by prayer and
supplication with thanksgiving let your requests be made known
unto God. Philippians 4:6

We lived in Thailand for one full year without a single money concern. We had no paying job, no stipend, no fundraising, no online side gig. Nothing was bringing in income. We did come with a chunk of money from the sale of our house but moving across the world, purchasing a vehicle, and setting up a household for a fair number of people isn't free. We went through what we brought very quickly.

And so for the remaining months of that first year, we were entirely dependent on what God provided. We still are. But it struck me that the moment we'd passed the one year mark, God allowed the honeymoon period to abruptly end.

August 30, 2020 was our first anniversary here and we'd just taken in our 6th Thai child less than a week earlier. We needed to head out on a very costly visa run to Chiang Mai. Our financial planning would probably give many people hives because, essentially, we *don't* plan.

If there's a need for a thing, and we have the funds available, we don't even consider not meeting the need. We don't consult our budget because it's non-existent. How does one create a budget when one doesn't have a clue how much there will be to work with from one month to the next? It's impossible. I know because we spent a few months trying and just ended up fighting from the stress of it.

We finally gave up as we realized God was asking us to be wise stewards of what we had, but to hold nothing back for tomorrow.

The whole concept flies in the face of everything we're told as young people when we launch into adulthood. We've had quite the learning curve, and we're still trying to overcome feeling like irresponsible teenagers living this way.

We were headed to immigration, praying for one year extensions, while also knowing our bank account was about to bottom out.

Covid worked in our favor in that particular situation, and the process had never been easier. They wanted people in and out so it took maybe an hour and we were on our way, albeit with drastically reduced padding in our pockets. We weren't worried, though. The money hadn't run out and so we just sort of figured we'd snuck under the radar and wouldn't experience the seasons of financial drought we'd heard about from other missionaries.

Fast forward less than a week, however, and the money had indeed run out. We had none left. We had food to provide and two employees to pay. It wasn't looking good and we were squirming more than I'd like to admit.

A card arrived in the mail with a check and the timing was clearly providential. We thanked our friends profusely, told them how God had used them (they'd sent the card more than a month earlier), and carried on.

But then that money ran out, too.

Interestingly, during this time we were also proceeding with the paperwork to rent an office for a language school and church plant. We'd been praying about the possibility since the beginning of the year when the pandemic hit, and while we'd almost rented the building in March, we tabled the idea due to the uncertainty everywhere. Now things had settled and we knew God was asking us to move forward. The month of September was spent attempting to make contact with the owner and then coming to an agreement.

As the month wore on and the financial deficit we were facing was becoming more uncomfortable, we began to question if perhaps we'd heard God wrong. Maybe we were running ahead of Him and He was having to pull out the stops to hold us back. We nearly caved and put the whole thing on hold, but then the conviction would settle on us again and we'd keep moving forward.

With $1500 USD due for the deposit in less than a week, not to mention all our bills for the month of October on top of it, we ran out of money yet again.

This time we looked at each other and agreed we needed to head to the park up the road, just Robbie and I, to pray for discernment. We were still wondering if maybe God was saying something we were stubbornly not hearing. And so we left the children in the care of our older girls for a few hours, and rode to the park.

While there, Robbie got a text from some of the dearest supporters of our ministry, saying they'd just sent a PayPal with $200. It's worth mentioning here that we'd said nothing of our need.

God had compelled them and they'd simply responded. But He wasn't finished. Because while the $200 got us through the month with some leftover, it wasn't enough to cover the needed deposit money.

But then, in the eleventh hour, we got a message from the home office saying a donation of $5000 had just come in. We'd also received other funds that covered our usual bills, which meant we went from broke, to suddenly having enough for the deposit PLUS some to get started furnishing the building with that which was needed.

He's never too soon and He's never too late.

In the months since we took possession of the building that we call The Mission Post, we've moved to a property to begin establishing and developing a licensed home for at-risk children. And being two unqualified people, with a larger-than-average family and zero business sense, there have been a few times where we've questioned the wisdom in maintaining and ministering from both places.

But always we look back, remember His provision, and know He'll provide not only the finances to keep going, but also the energy, help, and resources.

He has yet to prove us wrong!

Discussion prompt: Scripture tells us our greatest danger is forgetting how God has led in the past. Take a few minutes to discuss ways in which you've seen God pulling off the impossible to keep the path clear before you.

Twenty-three

*Now the Lord had said unto Abram, Get thee out of thy country,
and from thy kindred, and from thy father's house, unto a land that
I will shew thee . . . So Abram departed, as the Lord had spoken
unto him. Genesis 12:1, 4*

Some days I ache for what is no longer. For the days I can't get back, the life I no longer possess, and the home which will never again be.

I miss the quiet life I didn't even realize was quiet. I long to be near enough all of my children that I can see them for holidays or even spontaneous visits. I want what I can't have, while also wanting what I *can*.

Lately we've been witnessing a battle waging in two of the three little boys we brought with us. The months have been hard on them as we've opened our home to children who haven't had the benefit of being raised in love or trained in obedience. They've heard cuss words slung, in both Thai and English, and witnessed more than their share of tantrums.

Before coming here, a tantrum in any of our three littlest boys was unheard of. They didn't always obey with perfection, obviously, but they never talked back or mouthed off or pitched a fit. And while they still don't throw tantrums or blatantly talk back, they were in no way prepared for the onslaught of what they'd experience here.

And some days my heart just hurts for their loss of innocence.

I sometimes want so badly to go back to our 3 acres on the mountain with the little stream that babbled along the lower portion of the property. I want the easy days of watching them jump into that shallow water, squealing and giggling with delight. Or listening to their sweet voices calling out to show me a minnow or crawdad they'd caught. I want that simplicity and I want back what the past year has stolen from them.

But then I'm reminded of how Abraham departed without question. He was given instructions, vague though they seem to have been, and he obeyed. Sometimes I think I'd have it easier if God had promised me the same as He'd promised Abram, however. Because God told him He'd make of him a great nation.

I just want the promise that my children will all come out of this intact. I've heard God encourage but I haven't heard Him promise.

I'm tired from the months, that are turning into years, where I haven't seen the faces of my older boys. I feel drained from missing them and wondering what it'll be like when they marry and have children while I live across the world. I try not to let my mind go there, but there are days where it happens before I catch myself.

I'm weary from the transition of *having* a church to *being* the church. I'm so grateful for the little church family God is building in a dark city, while also missing the big church family we've left behind. We had so many friends, and so much spiritual support all around us, but I realize now we largely took it for granted. We didn't understand how blessed we were to have likeminded people to do life with in every direction we turned. That experience is slowly being built back although primary with people we don't share a language or culture with. It's slower and more awkward, but every bit as powerful.

I remember hearing a sermon years ago where a lego was used to symbolize a person. The message went on to demonstrate that there's only so many pegs on a lego where you can fit another lego. And because people come with a limited capacity to invest deeply in the lives of others, we tend to shift our legos around throughout the various seasons of life. Meaning that someone we are close friends with right now, and whose lego is firmly snapped to ours, might later move away. Rather than being able to maintain that deep and meaningful connection with so much physical distance between us, we shift them off our lego to make room for another.

Only so many legos fit at one time before we're overwhelmed.

And so finding ourselves moved off the legos of dear friends and even family … not because they don't care or because we no longer matter, but because that's the way humanity naturally functions … has been hard. It hurts. We mostly don't think about it but then something happens or something is said and a wave of grieve falls over us.

And because we now live on a different continent, in a new culture where we're mostly stared at for being different (we live in a part of Thailand where there are only a very few white-skinned foreigners), it's not like we've just moved to a different state where we can easily rebuild what's been lost.

I don't share this to elicit sympathy, or pity, but to offer a real picture of what your missionary friends serving in foreign lands may be going through. They need prayed for, encouraged, loved, and reminded God still sees them. They're likely battling guilt over missing what they've left behind while also being fully committed to what God has put before them. When they have a hard day or a difficult year, they often don't have a physically present support group to help them navigate it all.

Supporting a missionary is more than sending a check, although don't ever underestimate the way your financial support of their ministry helps them feel trusted and cared for. It gives them a sense of partnership and works to soften the effects of them feeling so alone and in over their heads.

But the tiniest thing, like a text or voice message or a letter in the mail or the reminder that you're praying for them can take a day that feels lonely, and turn it into one that doesn't.

I'd love to know Abraham's full story. I'd love to get to know what he felt, what he and Sarah talked about, how they struggled as sojourners for all the remaining years of their lives. I'd love to know about the times they cried out, asking God why and yet determining to keep their eyes forward. Because while they lived to see their promised child be born and grow into a young man, they didn't live to see the great nation God had promised to make of him.

They could only choose to believe what they couldn't yet see. We are just exactly the same.

Discussion prompt: Nobody is spared loss or some sort of grief. Our experiences all look different but that doesn't make one more and one less. What has God asked of you that has required you to continually surrender your will to His?

Twenty-four

But the Lord said unto Samuel, Look not on his countenance, or on the height of his stature; because I have refused him: for the Lord seeth not as man seeth; for man looketh on the outward appearance, but the Lord looketh on the heart. 1 Samuel 16:7

We'd been in Thailand less than 6 months when we met him. A friend in our village made the introductions and things moved swiftly from there.

A Buddhist monk and a Mexican-American Christian aren't the likeliest of pairs, yet my husband and his orange-robe-clad sidekick forged a friendship that has grown by the week. Ram is a staple around our property now and can be seen, on any given day, quietly tending the two water buffalo he keeps here.

At first it was a mutually beneficial arrangement; Ram wanted to improve his English and learn some Spanish and Robbie was helping him with both. We wanted to learn about Buddhism, the teachings, and the culture. Being a monk, there seemed no better source from which to draw our information.

But as the weeks went by, it became less about what we could get from each other and more about the fact that we just enjoyed the relationship. Ram is kind-hearted, easy-going, and accepting of our differences. He never tries to make Buddhists out of us and goes out of his way to help us fit into his culture without ever trying to get us to compromise our beliefs.

We've spent hours in the truck together, him in the front seat with Robbie, while I ride in the back with the children. And we talk. We ask questions and he provides answers. *He* asks questions, and *we* provide answers. We share our experiences, we help each other out, and we broaden our perspectives as the wall between religions/cultures seem less of a barrier than they had previously.

We've learned afresh, through this friendship with "our monk", that sharing the gospel isn't approaching a person and shoving what you know about God onto them. It's about investing in a relationship, where you genuinely care about the other person, and allow God to provide opportunities for you to testify of His character and love. We've had countless opportunities to do so and while he's still dressed in orange, walking around barefoot, and living at the temple, seeds have been planted that wouldn't have been if we'd held him at an arm's distance.

But also, God has used this precious soul to help us in so many ways it's hard to keep count.

Our first English students at The Mission Post bravely ventured in at Ram's suggestion. Some of the first elderly people we began to visit, and provide food for, came at his introduction.

He entered our church plant/English school and sat boldly in front of the big windows, talking with us, causing natural prejudices against the foreigner missionaries to be abandoned. We have no way of knowing, this side of heaven, just how many people have seen him enter that building and, as a result, decide we aren't something to be afraid of.

A few weeks ago, Robbie was attempting to register a motorbike we'd acquired. It should have been an easy task but because we aren't Thai nationals, it was anything *but* easy. He was repeatedly told he didn't have the right paperwork and was sent from one building to the other and back again.

A day or two of this passed and no headway was gained. Ram told Robbie he wanted to go with him. He figured he could help translate and was hopeful the paperwork could finally be completed. And so Robbie went by the temple and Ram hopped in the truck.

But when they got to the first office, they were sent to the other. In short order, Ram realized there was blatant prejudice against Robbie because he was a foreigner. In fact, one lady actually said to Ram, "How do we know he's not a terrorist with a bomb in that bag?"

Ram isn't one to lose control of himself, and so he calmly raised a hand and began pointing a finger at her, telling her emphatically that she was wrong for even thinking in such a way. He reprimanded her for the bias, and unfounded judgement she had passed on a man who just wanted to follow the law and register a bike. He made his voice heard and she hung her head in shame.

They ended that day with the paperwork nobody would give Robbie before, because a monk had taken up for his Christian friend. The unlikliest of friendships in a country where about 1% of the population is professing Christian.

Many centuries ago, God spoke to Samuel, warning him not to look on the outward appearance because he'd deem a man ready who God knew was not. But the flip side of that is true, as well. Because how often do we *discount* the value of a person based on our flawed perception of the situation?

We never imagined coming here and having God use a monk to open the way for His word to spread. And yet, that's exactly what He's done.

We have no way of knowing if one day Ram will open his heart and mind to our God, and really it's none of our business. Our job isn't to save people, it's to provide an opportunity for them to encounter Jesus, through obedience to the Spirit. The rest is out of our hands.

But as we walk that out, what a blessing it is to find the most unexpected friends in the most unexpected places.

Discussion prompt: Who in your life can you think of that God has placed there in the unlikeliest of ways or timing?

Twenty-five

For ye have need of patience, that, after ye have done the will of God, ye might receive the promise. Hebrews 10:36

I'm a wallflower of the worst kind. I'd prefer to be invisible as opposed to being seen.

Which is strange then, that I would so willingly move to a country where I may never again move about undetected. Because if we've never met in person, allow me to give you a quick description of myself.

I'm of Irish-German-American descent and I have glowing white skin, freckles and not-straight-but-not-curly hair that acts like a petulant child in humidity. And Sukhothai, Thailand is 365 days of humidity. I have a brood of children that run the spectrum of skin colors, and a laugh that emits way too loudly when I feel awkward. None of these things begets the quiet life of a wallflower.

When Robbie first began traveling around on a motorbike, I was scared to ride with him. Scared because I detest motorized *anything* that only has two wheels. But when I finally strapped on a helmet and hopped on the back, I found my fear of wrecking overtaken by my distaste for all the people looking at the white girl on the motorbike. Robbie, being half Mexican, has brown skin so he doesn't stand out quite so much. I can't express how jealous I am of him for that simple reason.

We pulled up in our van to a 7-11 one day and Robbie ran inside to grab bottles of water. Our American boys and our youngest Thai girl, Fahsai, were in the back and Zachy, our 6 year old, was doing his usual: waving out the windows to the passerby who were gawking in at his pale skin and unruly, blonde thatch of hair. Before I knew it, a group had gathered around our van and people were talking to the children. They were posing for selfies with the *farangs* and taking videos, which I have no doubt made an appearance on social media. It was hilarious and yet had me so far out of my comfort zone that I had to check myself to see if this was really my life.

It was, and still is.

Our building in town, The Mission Post, is located in the business district inside the city of Sukhothai. It's on a busy street with a roundabout and other offices all around. Directly across the narrow, one-way street from us is a motorbike repair shop. Two men, one older and one younger, sit out there all day, 6 days a week. Almost without fail, they are there when we arrive and also when we leave.

The younger of the two is a handsome, clean-cut man with the biggest smile you've ever seen. For the first few weeks, we just thought he was an extremely happy guy who finds incredible fulfilment in fixing broken motorbikes. And I still believe that may be the case.

But beyond that, he seems to derive an uncanny pleasure in watching our every move. If you happen to glance out the window, about 90% of the time you'll find him staring inside while his hands seem to mindlessly move over the broken part of the bike on which he's working. And quite often, you also see him laughing. To be entirely honest, I'd have to admit my feelings about this man have run the gamut. His smile is contagious. He doesn't seem shady or give off a "vibe" that causes one to be apprehensive of ill intent. He just genuinely seems amused by the activity of this lively group of pale-skinned people who teach English and have Christian church services across the road.

But it has tested the endurance of my patience to be watched by him. I can't even begin to convince myself I'm invisible when every move we make is under his direct scrutiny.

The other day we arrived at the office. Nik was still sore from his motorbike wreck and he hobbled out of the van, being careful of the wounds all over his arms and legs. And as I opened the truck to pull a few things out to carry inside, the older man spoke up. He said, in Thai, "Do you speak Thai?" I heard him and turned around to indicate I understood. He then asked, "What happened to the tall guy?"

I answered and explained he'd had a wreck on his motorbike which is where all the cuts and scrapes had come from. He nodded his head while the younger guy burst out into wild laughter. It wasn't mean spirited, it was just clear he found it more than a little amusing the big American had bit it on the road and was now back to being transported in the truck his mom drives.

But while these encounters are always uncomfortable, they aren't without value.

Because I'm slowly learning to be less protective of my pride. I'm becoming increasingly less fearful of what other people think or of how they might assess me. I'm more aware of the importance of my resting face being friendly, and thanks to the masked world we now live in, my smile reaching all the way to my eyes.

I'm seeing that the more I focus on myself, even if it's just to keep myself from *being* focused on, the less my eyes are on Jesus or my mind is on others. God has plucked me out of my comfortable and plopped me into a situation where my carnal self is crossed daily in order to teach me the old man must die.

I'm grateful He saw me worth fighting for because I know how exhausting a stubborn, self-consumed child is to raise. He could have taken the easy path and just tossed me aside as too great a project and chosen someone else instead. But that's not who He is.

He sees each of us, in all our weakness and pride, and does everything He can to draw us into His transforming presence. He lets us squirm more than we'd like but only because He knows the squirming is the result of the purifying fire.

And one day, we'll be able to look back and see, every uncomfortable moment was worth it.

Discussion prompt: Generally, a life surrendered to God will be accompanied by uncomfortable circumstances. What is something you've gone, or are going, through that you know God is using to purify your character?

Twenty-six

For we have not an high priest which cannot be touched with the feeling of our infirmities; but was in all points tempted like as we are, yet without sin. Hebrews 4:15

Our first two Thai children, Wind and Sky, came to us a month and a half after we arrived in Thailand. We'd been in Sukhothai for only two weeks, when we found ourselves going out to buy beds for this boy/girl sibling set. And we had 8 months to learn the ropes before we received a second call for help.

It was a time we needed, although we didn't realize the gift of those months at the time.

In June of 2020, several months into the pandemic, we received a call from our friend Josh. He and his wife have a ministry caring for young people about 5 hours from us in Chiang Mai and they adopted Wind and Sky's older sister, Praew, into their family several years earlier. He was calling to say there was a boy in need of a home and wanted to know if we were open to taking him in.

We said we were and the call ended.

Over the next several days, it became clear the little boy would be coming with a younger sister. She was only three and we were excited by the idea of such a young one since she would surely be easier to train out of the unsavory habits with which she'd almost certainly come to us.

A few weeks passed and we got the call that they'd be arriving that morning. We scurried around preparing and not too long later, the vehicle pulled in and they got out. That day marked a whole new beginning. One we couldn't have predicted if we'd tried.

Because young though she was, she was hard and determined. We lived in a small village and her screams would pierce through the walls and we'd run around trying to close windows to prevent our neighbors from thinking we were torturing her. She would thrash and scream for an hour or more with no sign of exhaustion. We often questioned each other how she could carry on so long without losing her voice or hurting herself so badly that she was compelled to stop.

It was a mystery we still cannot solve.

About six months after they arrived, we moved from that village to the 24 rai (9 1/2 acre) property we've now made home. And we fully expected that the move would bring with it a bit of reprieve from her raging. She'd have more space where she could expend her angry energy. We shouldn't have been so hopeful.

The move seemed to rattle her and she was a suddenly on edge more than ever before. The slightest misstep by *anyone*, and she was set off. Our first two Bible Workers had moved to the property with us, and it was horrifying to have people so up close and personal listening to the shrieks that branded us as tyrannical parents. Stressful cannot *begin* to describe those first months after moving.

We settled into the new normal, got better acquainted with Sneh and Waew (our Bible Workers), and began to accept that this little girl may never stop screaming. And then suddenly, several months in, she made radical strides in a promising direction.

Don't mistake me for saying she stopped getting angry over seemingly nothing or that the fits ceased to be part and parcel of daily life. But things calmed to a more manageable level. Let me open the door of transparency to you and admit we've had a seriously rough go.

We've cried, complained, ranted, and threatened to throw in the towel. We've not held our patience with the grace and meekness we should have, and we've questioned if we were even cut out for this work. We want to serve but apparently only when it doesn't cross our will so consistently. Only when it doesn't require our nerves to be shattered day in and day out.

And only when those we're serving don't slap us in the face for trying to help them.

But then my mind goes to Jesus. Isn't this exactly what He endured. Did He not pour Himself out, far more extensively and with perfect love, only to be spat on and rejected? Did they not falsely accuse Him, misunderstand Him, endlessly badger Him, and try to trap Him? Did He not endure everything, and more, than we ever will in all our years?

He did, because He *had* to. But He also had to, because He *wanted* to. There could be nothing we'd encounter that Satan could accuse Him of not covering with His sacrifice. All the t's were crossed and the i's were all dotted. He was tempted in *all points tempted like as we are.*

Only He endured it all without sinning.

That's the experience I want. To be so hid in Christ that I'm not consumed trying to protect myself from the things that don't *feel* good. I want to come face to face with a screaming, tantrum throwing child and see myself in her. I want to recognize I'm no better or easier to shepherd. I want to see her disheveled hair, tear-stained face, and wrinkled brow and know she is me.

Not because I want to *be* what I see in her, but because the only way I can heal from the fact that I *am*, is to recognize my need. As she's slowly softening, I want to, as well. I want my heart to be opened more with the rising of each day's sun.

If He endured it, I want to, as well.

Discussion prompt: Can you identify a person, or people, in your life that God is using to chisel your rough edges? How do respond to them? How does He?

Twenty-seven

And whosoever doth not bear his cross, and come after me, cannot be my disciple. For which of you, intending to build a tower, sitteth not down first, and counteth the cost, whether he have sufficient to finish it? Lest haply, after he hath laid the foundation, and is not able to finish it, all that behold it begin to mock him, Saying, This man began to build, and was not able to finish. Luke 14:27-30

It wasn't long after moving to the children's home property that we began to get a vision for what we believed God was asking us to do. Incomplete, and deteriorating structures, would be brought to new life.

A building that was partially complete, seemed almost to be *asking* to be made over into the first phase of a school. The decision to move forward was easy and the transformational work got underway.

An unstable wall had to be knocked down and built back with integrity. Nearly everything needed plastering, inside and out, and doorways and window frames had to be built. The floor had to be leveled and a ceiling needed to be hung. At first the progress seemed swift and I think we all expected it to be finished pretty quickly.

We realized the construction, in addition to everything else which needed to be done around the property, was more than our small staff could handle. God provided workers from around the community who came in and added their expertise to the project. Things would start swinging and picking up speed, and the end seemed nearer every day.

Finally the time came where the floors had been laid, the ceiling was in place, the plastering had been completed, the windows installed, and the three extra bathrooms right outside had been built. We got so close that a break seemed in order.

And so we began tending to other things. Nobody got lazy or unproductive, but the focus shifted and the schoolhouse settled comfortably onto the back burner. So close and yet so far from completion.

A few weeks passed without much progress until it really started to nag at us. We'd see the nearly-finished building and be reminded it still wasn't functional. It had unpainted walls, no electricity, no doors, and no screen for the vented areas where mosquitos would easily make their way into every nighttime gathering. The big stuff had happened with some speed and efficiency, but somehow the detail work wasn't quite so compelling.

I don't like unfinished projects and this one certainly bothered me. But it also served to show me how very similar we are in our Christian experiences. We embrace the gospel, accept Christ, and begin to learn of His character. As we do, He shows us "big" things in our lives that aren't consistent with being His follower. And so we get to work letting Him remove them from our shelf of habits.

We clean up our language, we put away drugs, and we turn from promiscuity. We tackle the big stuff, you know? And while no sin habit generally dies without a battle, *sometimes* the big ones are the easiest. The problem is, that while it may not be socially acceptable to be a prostitute at the same time you're professing to be a Christian, it *is* generally acceptable to continue watching violent action movies or reading romance novels or engaging in gossip. So we aren't as quick to address those things that other Christians seem unconcerned by.

But if we're truly seeking Christ, eventually He'll succeed in communicating the need for further purification and forward progress will be made. At which point, the things we're watching, and listening to, and talking about will be addressed and we'll find ourselves surrendering in those areas, too.

Which then leaves a person in a similar condition as how our little schoolhouse stands right now; *so close and yet so far away.*

Because the time has come for the serious *detail* work to commence. The obvious has been dealt with and is no longer plaguing us. Oh, we may slip back on occasion, but generally we know to grab hold of Christ before we sink any further. And the reality is, the detail work is the work of a lifetime.

It isn't a once and done, it's a continual abiding. It's being at the place where you're learning to hear and discern His voice with greater willingness and determination. It's a deepening desire to not offend God in even your thoughts.

The problem is, it's tempting to get to that place and then camp out right at the threshold, without ever crossing over. It's where so many of us get hung up wanting to *be* Christians without knowing Christ. Because to truly know Him is to reflect Him, and to reflect Him is to surrender *everything*.

We've given ourselves the kick in the pants needed to resume the detail work on our school. The wiring is nearly finished, paint is going up, and doors are being hung. Soon the screen will be in place and we'll be able to move the piano into the chapel and begin having group worships there. It's taking discipline with more interesting things calling for our time and attention, but the push to bring the project to completion is on.

And as each finishing touch is made, I can only pray that we will do the same in our spiritual lives. That we won't one day stand before God and hear Him say, "This man began to build, and was not able to finish."

By the grace of God, we want to instead hear the words, *"Well done, thou good and faithful servant: thou hast been faithful over a few things, I will make thee ruler over many things: enter thou into the joy of thy lord."* (Matthew 25:21)

Discussion prompt: Where are you in this journey to "completion"? Have you allowed yourself to stall out somewhere while God stands calling you forward? Are you willing to get back in the fight?

Twenty-eight

And thine ears shall hear a word behind thee, saying, This is the way, walk ye in it, when ye turn to the right hand, and when ye turn to the left. Isaiah 30:21

Less than a month after moving to Sukhothai, Robbie made a trip to Chiang Mai leaving me home with just Hannah, Levi, Quinn, and Zach. We had no transportation and so on the second or third day, we got a little stir crazy and decided to attempt walking to the park. I consulted with Robbie about it by phone, and he believed it was close enough to easily get there on foot. So we started out.

However, we weren't yet acclimated (at all!!) to the heat and Levi was only about a month out from his 5 day hospital stay following a serious asthma attack. What we had expected to be a short walk was far from it. Levi was holding steady but my gut was telling me he wasn't going to make the whole trip without meeting with struggle. The problem at that point was, it was about as far to go back as it was to go forward.

Right about the time I was attempting to decide what to do, a man and his son popped out of an alley right in front of us. He spoke a little English and asked me where we were going. I did my best to explain, and he did his best to tell me it was too far to walk. He motioned toward his truck, which we hadn't even noticed, sitting in the middle of the road. He was clearly asking us to hop in the back.

If there's one thing I'm not, it's a hitchhiker. I'm not a risk-taker, nor am I an adventurer. I'd do anything, however, before I'd put my kids in danger. And so what happened next still shocks me to my core.

Because we climbed up and in. I had absolute peace that God had sent this man at the exact moment we needed help. And He was so kind as to have the man's young son along to make it easier to avoid seeing him as the threat my natural response would normally see him as.

So we settled in and began the ride to the park. Hannah kept looking at me as though trying to figure out who I was and if I'd lost my mind. Finally we exchanged a glance and cracked up laughing over the absurdity of the unlikely situation.

A few minutes later, the pickup pulled into the parking lot of our intended destination and the man hopped out and began helping the little boys down. I thanked him and asked how much he'd like to be paid for the ride. He quickly patted his chest over his heart and said, "No money! I happy, I happy!". I thanked him again and he climbed back in his truck and drove away.

We gathered in a circle and prayed our thanks to God for providing for us in such a unique way and then spent a few hours letting the boys play while Hannah and I talked. By the time we went to leave, all the water bottles were drained but the air had only cooled by a degree or two. I knew we were now faced with a similar problem going back and voiced to Hannah that I didn't think God was going to allow us to make the trip by foot.

Of course, I had no idea how He planned to prevent it because I certainly wasn't about to ask anyone for a ride. We prayed again, thanking God for being with us.

And then we started the trip back, a little slower this time to preserve our energy. The boys were happy and singing but the heat was oppressive. We didn't get very far at all, when we suddenly saw a car pull over to the side of the road and stop. I looked at Hannah and knew we were both wondering the same thing.

Was God already providing us another ride?

The car remained where it was until we came upon it, and as we began to pass by, the gentleman inside asked where we were going. I motioned to tell him and he told us to get in. It was unbelievable. Not only because a second man was offering us a ride in a single day, but because I had peace all over again that it was safe to accept.

We squeezed in and he delivered us safely to the shop I'd indicated that was close to our house. We got out, thanked him, and he drove off. We walked the last little bit home and again thanked God.

It's been more than 18 months since that day and we've walked along roads many, many times. Never once has anybody stopped to ask where we're going or to offer us a ride. Not once.

I don't share this to be reckless or to encourage anyone to start taking rides from strangers. I share it to convey the truth that when we're connecting with Christ, and listening for His voice, He will direct us where to go, when, and how.

We'll hear the word behind us saying, "This is the way, walk ye in it, when ye turn to the right hand, and when ye turn to the left."

And even if it seems to be directing us in a path contrary to the one we'd naturally choose, we're never safer than when we obey and walk therein. I learned that day God sometimes provides help in ways we wouldn't ask and don't expect. If fear had stood in the way of my accepting His help, Levi may well have had an asthma attack.

I'm thankful to this day that God enabled me to follow where He was leading with perfect peace!

Discussion prompt: Do you remember a time when God asked you to do something that seemed irresponsible, yet you knew He was leading? How did you respond?

Twenty-nine

Wherefore, my beloved brethren, let every man be swift to hear, slow to speak, slow to wrath: For the wrath of man worketh not the righteousness of God. James 1:19-20

Nearly 20 years ago we attended a family retreat. It was the kind of gathering where people brought campers, or tents, or rented cabins and stayed for the week of meetings. We had signed up to attend with another family and had agreed to share two sides of the same cabin.

The night of the first meeting I realized I was out of my parenting league. In front of me were rows of families with small children who sat still and quiet for nearly two hours. Mine had stayed at the cabin to be put to bed that night while I attended the meeting, and I suddenly found myself dreading the next day.

My inadequacies as a mother were about to be put on display.

Morning dawned and my energetic little boys woke with their usual enthusiasm for life. I got the older two settled with breakfast and then tended to my baby. We hadn't even neared the meetinghouse yet and I could feel the tension rising. Every word they spoke sounded too loud and every move they made seemed too erratic. I snapped at them to calm down but, while they tried, they hadn't been trained to control themselves in the way I was suddenly requiring.

An hour or so later, with hair combed and faces shiny, we walked over to the first meeting. Finding seats toward the back, we settled in, hoping for the best. Because we had done cursory training, they made it for about 20 minutes before beginning to squirm and start whispering. We did our best to gently quiet and reposition them so they might settle back in. They weren't bad but they weren't as "good" as those other kids.

The irritation that had begun earlier in the morning took a death hold on me.

I began to be more firm in my requests for silence and stillness. Gone was the smile I'd plastered on my face less than 30 minutes before. I was daring them with my eyes to cross me and they were accepting the challenge. The angrier I got the less obedient they were. They weren't scared of me and they seemed not to be inclined to please right then, either.

The meeting finally ended and I marched them resolutely back to the cabin. I placed them not-so-gently on their beds and proceeded to tell them all the ways they'd failed to perform. My spirit was ugly and my motive was worse. I was more concerned with them embarrassing me, and exposing my parenting weaknesses, than I was about the spiritual foundation (or lack thereof) they were being given. It's a hideous memory that still plagues me and I don't know if I've ever been brave enough to ask if they remember it.

Those three little boys, more so even than the two girls who quickly followed, survived the brunt of my *experimental* years.

Because while I tried Christian living and mothering on for size, when I'd find it too snug for my liking, I'd just let out the seams a little. I wanted to make room within the garment Christ was offering me, without actually having to fit inside it.

Living in conflict with my conscience like this caused me so much unnecessary frustration. I truly loved my kids, and genuinely threw myself into raising them well, but I was so misguided in my efforts. I've repented, and I know God has forgiven me. By His amazing grace, I have an incredible relationship with each of my now-grown children. But none of that negates the impact my damaging approach left on them.

Fourteen years after my first child was born, and almost 7 years after my fifth, I delivered twin boys. I was given a fresh opportunity to make better decisions from infancy. I was so grateful.

The several years leading up to the birth of the twins were fairly traumatic for our family and my hold on God had been significantly broken. Those two babies were the lifeline God threw me. He knew nothing would motivate me to take hold of Him again like knowing *seven* children now depended on me. An 8th child was born into our arms 3 years later.

It's been a slow, but steady, path forward and God has shown me the importance of purposefully reflecting His character and patiently allowing them the growth process God intends us all to follow.

It's been so interesting to see how much easier it is for the last 3 little guys to grasp who Jesus is than it was for our first 5 children. Not because God has made Himself clearer to them, but because I haven't been *quite so grossly* misrepresenting Him. I'm a little quicker to hear, slower to speak, and slower to grow angry with them. I don't measure their behavior by whether it embarrasses me or not but rather I'm learning to invest in it by holding them *equally accountable,* no matter the circumstance. I still have a high standard but, as I commit myself each day to God, He helps me balance my expectations with love and long-suffering.

I've watched God working to redeem the years the locusts had eaten with my older children, and while I hurt for the extra spiritual challenges I've caused them, I know He is the redeemer of souls. I see Him at work in each of their lives.

By His grace, one day I'll be able to stand before Him and present every one of my now 14 children, having not lost a single one. Nothing inspires me to keep putting one foot in front of the other more than that.

Nothing!

Discussion prompt: Is spontaneous anger or a quick temper something you struggle with? Is it something you've learned to surrender?

Thirty

And Jonathan said to the young man that bare his armour, Come, and let us go over unto the garrison of these uncircumcised: it may be that the Lord will work for us: for there is no restraint to the Lord to save by many or by few. 1 Samuel 14:6

I love this verse so much. It's packed with both power and promise and there's so many spiritual lessons to be drawn from it. Interestingly, the story it takes my mind to is a true one and it involves our friend who just so happens to also be named Jonathan.

He's an American missionary to Thailand and currently serves, with his wife, as foreign corespondents who create videos to share real-life stories from the field.

This particular event happened 6 or 7 years ago as Jonathan was traveling with another missionary named, Travis. They were headed through the jungle to Travis' school where Jonathan planned to capture, through video, what was happening there. They stopped for the night at the home of a friend of Travis'. Having laid out mats on the floor, both young men went to sleep.

But around midnight, Jonathan woke to the extremely painful sensation of something being on his back. As he was shaking out of his sleep, he swatted a hand at it, but whatever it was didn't move. He swatted again and this time the pain let up a bit and he heard something moving away from him.

His first thought was the need to know what it was that bit him, so he grabbed a flashlight and looked around. Finally, the light landed on a snake. Now if you've heard anything about snakes in Thailand, you'd know he had considerable cause for concern at this point. Jonathan had heard of snakes that would bite people and they'd be dead before they took two steps. He stood in the dark of that room, nowhere near help, wondering if he was about to die.

He prayed the only desperate prayer his mind could conjure up in the moment: "Lord, help me!" And then he moved to wake up Travis. Being the dead of night, Travis didn't awaken easily, but a moment or two later he stirred into consciousness. Jonathan quickly informed him the matter was serious and that he'd just been bitten by a snake.

Travis snapped out of the cloud of sleep he'd been in and yelled out in a whisper to confirm what he'd heard.

Jonathan pulled down the neckline of his shirt and Travis saw nothing. He suggested that Jonathan had dreamed the whole thing. But then they raised the back of his shirt and the bite became visible. Much to the relief of both men, the mark Travis saw indicated the snake hadn't been venomous. He suggested they both go back to sleep.

Venomous or not, Jonathan was dealing with an adrenaline surge and a return to sleep didn't come easy. Additionally, he could feel venom stinging him like a bee right over his spine. He convinced himself it was his imagination running haywire, praised God for His protection, and eventually drifted off. He woke the next morning to the happy thought that he was, indeed, still alive!

They took the opportunity to have Travis check out his back now that there was better light and once he got a look at it, he sat without saying anything. Obviously, Jonathan picked up on his change in demeanor and asked him what was wrong.

Travis told him he saw two fang marks. The snake had, in fact, been venomous. Later, Jonathan had a chance to look through a book of snakes and identified only one that looked like the one he'd seen that night.

It was a cobra.

Jonathan hadn't been a random victim of a snake bite, he'd been the target of a very intentional attack. Satan did not want the work God was doing at Travis' school being shown or told to others, and he knew that was Jonathan's intent. God did what God does: He sustained His workers while they were about His work.

We try so hard to find the safest place, or the most secure course, or the least risky option. We look with finite eyes trying to discern things God has deemed it's not our business to know just yet. Sometimes He only points to the narrow path and promises it's the safest one.

And just like it says in 1 Samuel 14:6, it doesn't matter if God has to defend us against many or few. It doesn't matter if the threat is weak or it's mighty. When we're abiding under the shadow of the Almighty, we have no need to fear the pestilence that walketh in darkness.

Even if it bites you.

Discussion prompt: How have you experienced God's deliverance from seeming hopelessness? Discuss some times you nearly caved to fear or intimidation and yet God proved He was stronger than the biggest threat to your life or peace.

Thirty-one

How then shall they call on him in whom they have not believed?
and how shall they believe in him of whom they have not heard?
and how shall they hear without a preacher? And how shall they
preach, except they be sent? as it is written, How beautiful are the
feet of them that preach the gospel of peace, and bring glad tidings of
good things! Romans 10:14,15

I was born in Germany on Thanksgiving eve of 1976. I speak no German, I left before I'd gathered even the trace of memory regarding the country, and I've never been back. I married a Mexican who was born in Alabama. And we're raising a brood of American-borne children in Thailand, alongside the 6 native children God placed in our care once arriving.

It's been a wild ride.

Scattered along the years between my birth and the present are many, many experiences I wish I'd been spared. Pain I'd prefer to never have known and decisions I wish I'd never have made. If I dwell on all that I very quickly believe myself beyond reach or rescue. Which is why I am constantly reminded by the Holy Spirit not to.

Instead, He shows me ways in which the things that happened through no fault of my own, have been used to add a dimension to my life I'd otherwise be missing. He reminds me of choices I made that reaped only heartache, He's masterfully used to give me empathy for the mistakes of others. And He keeps reaffirming the truth that the *pain* I wasn't spared was so I'd have compassion I couldn't possibly have known without it.

Even so, I sat toward the front of the church as Jon and Natalie spoke from the pulpit. They'd been invited to share, over the course of a weekend, the desperate need of the gospel throughout the 10/40 window and particularly in Asia.

They offered their experience from being over here and from the many experiences working closely with missionaries and Bible Workers for years. They told of people dying in darkness, having no knowledge of Christ. They told of people living in hopelessness, not understanding the gift of a Savior. But it wasn't their stories that shook me.

It was the absence of response I experienced as I listened.

I sat in that pew, tucked away with my husband and most of my children, and I felt *nothing*. Not the hint of a stirring. It was sickening.

The realization hit me toward the final meeting, that I was seriously deficient in empathy, compassion, and love. I had my comfortable family and my comfortable home. My husband had his comfortable jobs and we had our comfortable friends. We lived a relatively peaceful life on our comfortable mountain surrounded by the beauty of the Creator's creation.

We had it good and I didn't have a single inclination to give it up. Which is exactly why I did.

Because God showed me myself that weekend. He held a mirror up to me and I wasn't happy with the reflection I found there. I was floating through life, offering of myself only what didn't push me too far or require too much. I served others when it was convenient and I always checked my personal desires before committing to something that required a sacrifice of self.

But that isn't sacrifice at all.

The first definition for the word *sacrifice* in Merriam-Webster is the following: *an act of offering to a deity something precious.*

Is there anything more precious to us than self, really? Don't we even grow irritated with the ones we love most when they encroach on our preferences? God showed me that I had a choice. I could do things the easier, but slower, way and stay where I was geographically, allowing Him to work on my character and that of my family. Or I could take the harder, but faster, way and leave everything I knew to serve Him in the unknown.

He was promising to give me a love for the very people I

honestly cared nothing about. It's harsh to admit it but isn't that sometimes what it comes down to? Admitting the ugly truth so He can do a new thing. My heart still felt hard but I was ready to let Him have it.

God was speaking the same kind of message to my husband and, by what can only be described as a miracle, we were simultaneously convicted He was calling us out from our *comfortable*.

Neither of us experienced a sudden surge of love for an unknown people but we did both experience a desire to come to that point. It was enough for the moment. As we've been here, God has given us eyes to see, and hearts to feel, the pain of people we'd never had encountered if we hadn't come.

He's allowed us to walk with a child, tormented by demons, to the path of freedom as the Spirit fought on her behalf. He's given us grace to stand, unafraid, in the face of a pandemic just a few months after leaving our homeland. He preserved us from believing "home" was the safest place to ride it out, as well meaning people were suggesting. Perhaps that's why He gave us Wind and Sky so soon into our time here; to keep us from running. But He's enabled us to love and serve people, who are terrified of this virus, in perfect peace.

He's increasing our desire to pray, and teaching us to ask Him to break our hearts with what breaks His. And He's sustained us by providing us with the willingness to be some of the hands and feet bringing the gospel of peace to a people languishing without it.

Because they can't have the opportunity to believe in Him of whom they have not even heard.

Discussion prompt: Where is God calling you? At home or beyond, how is He asking you to serve?

Afterword

God has graciously allowed us to serve Him in two separate locations, doing two types of outreach.

Bˆān Tā Yîm translates into English as *Smiling Eyes Home*. We are currently in the process of securing licensing to allow this ministry to expand. We are planning the development of the property to hold a maximum capacity of 50-60 additional children, and the staff needed to keep the children well provided for.

We're also in the process of building a school, and securing the legal ability to educate those under our care, in the knowledge of Scripture and the admonition of the Lord. This project is far bigger than we are and will only become a reality through the guidance of the Holy Spirit and persevering prayer.

* * *

The Mission Post is our ministry office and church plant within the business district of the city of Sukhothai. We offer a selection of English language classes, food outreach ministry, and have begun the process of developing health and wellness programs for the community. The second floor of the building is the church and it's been a blessing to get to watch the number of people gathering here grow as God is pulling together a congregation of believers in this gospel-deprived country.

* * *

If you want to support our ministry for these precious children through financial contribution, you can visit https://www.wal kingredeemed.com/welcome/donate to see the ways you can do so.

You can also support our ministries through purchases made from our online store found at shopwalkingredeemed.com. There you'll find all our digital products and books, as well as a growing line of Christian t-shirts we've designed.

As always, we are abundantly grateful for your prayers on behalf of the Thai people!

About the Author

You can connect with me on:
- https://www.walkingredeemed.com
- https://www.facebook.com/walkingredeemed

www.ingramcontent.com/pod-product-compliance
Lightning Source LLC
Chambersburg PA
CBHW071627150726
48000CB00004B/1919